Terrorism

Short Histories of Big Ideas Series List

Published   *Capitalism* By Paul Bowles

Feminism By June Hannam

Environmentalism By David Peterson del Mar

Communism By Mark Sandle

Nationalism R.J.B. Bosworth

Available soon   *Fascism* Martin Blinkhorn

Zionism David Engel

Modernism Robin Walz

Colonialism Norrie Macqueen

Terrorism

ROSEMARY H.T. O'KANE

Harlow, England • London • New York • Boston • San Francisco • Toronto
Sydney • Tokyo • Singapore • Hong Kong • Seoul • Taipei • New Delhi
Cape Town • Madrid • Mexico City • Amsterdam • Munich • Paris • Milan

PEARSON EDUCATION LIMITED

Edinburgh Gate
Harlow CM20 2JE
United Kingdom
Tel: +44 (0)1279 623623
Fax: +44 (0)1279 431059
Website: www.pearsoned.co.uk

First edition published in Great Britain in 2007

ISBN: 978-0-582-50610-7

British Library Cataloguing in Publication Data
A CIP catalogue record for this book can be obtained from the British Library

Library of Congress Cataloging in Publication Data
A CIP catalogue record for this book can be obtained from the Library of Congress

10 9 8 7 6 5 4 3 2 1
11   10   09   08   07

Set by 35 in 9/15pt Iowan
Printed and bound in Malaysia

The Publisher's policy is to use paper manufactured from sustainable forests.

To Harriet

Contents

Preface   ix
Timeline   x

Chapter 1 Terrorism past and present   1

Chapter 2 The concept of terrorism   27

Chapter 3 Revolutionary reigns of terror   49

Chapter 4 Totalitarian regimes   71

Chapter 5 State terrorism at home and abroad   96

Chapter 6 Terrorist groups from within liberal
               democracies   120

Chapter 7 Terrorist groups and repressive regimes   143

Chapter 8 International terrorism   165

Chapter 9 The future of terrorism   187

References   193
Index   199

Preface

The word 'terrorism' conveys an image of the bomb under the park bench, of explosives carried in the rucksack of the suicide bomber and of hijacked aeroplanes. Today we live in a world in which such acts of terrorism regularly hit the news. To think of terrorism only in such ways, however, is to seriously misunderstand its true nature. Terrorism is far from being only the preserve of groups and individuals; it is also perpetrated by states and, at its most extreme, can identify regimes. A full understanding of terrorism can only be achieved by considering all these forms. This is my ambition here. For setting out on this journey of understanding I thank the editor of the series, Gordon Martel. Without his encouragement and help I doubt that the journey would have even begun, let alone progressed towards its destination. I thank him also for his patience; it took far longer than intended. I am also grateful, as always, to my family, Les and Harriet Rosenthal. They make it all worthwhile.

Timeline

1st century AD	Zealots-Sicarii oppose the Roman occupation of Judea in Ancient Palestine, for approximately 25 years; ends with mass suicide at Masada in 73 AD
1090–1275	The Assassins active in Turkish Seljuk Empire (in regions of today's Iran and Syria)
1200–1300	Thugs of India at their height; probably active from seventh to nineteenth century
1779	Lynch law first used (Virginia, USA)
1793–94	Jacobin Reign of Terror in France
1865	Ku Klux Klan forms in United States
1875	Development of gelignite
1876	'Propaganda by the deed' first advocated at the Anarchist International
1879	*Narodnaya Volya* (the People's Will) set up in Russia; ends 1894
1894	February: Emile Henry explodes a bomb in the Café Terminus, Paris
1915–16	The Armenian massacres
1916	Easter Rising in Dublin; Irish Volunteers becomes the Irish Republican Army (IRA) in 1919

1917–21	Revolutionary Reign of Terror in Russia; begins December 1917 with the setting up of the Cheka (disbanded February 1922)
1930–53	Stalin's Terror Regime in the Soviet Union; the GULAG set up, 1930; the Great Purges, 1936–38
1933–45	Hitler's Nazi Regime in Germany; *Kristallnacht* (Crystal Night), 9–10 November 1938, begins fully fledged terror regime; Holocaust begins 1941
1938	July: Irgun Zvai Leumi explodes land mines in an Arab fruit market in Haifa
1940	Lehi (the Stern Gang) breaks away from Irgun
1946	July: Irgun blows up the King David Hotel in Jerusalem
1954	Algerian National Liberation Front (FLN) forms; September 1956, sets up *Zone Autome d'Alger* (ZAA); 'Battle of Algiers' lasts until Autumn 1957
1955	Al-Fatah (Palestine National Liberation Movement) set up by Yasser Arafat
1959	*Euskadi 'ta Askatasuna* (Basque Homeland and Freedom, ETA) formed
1960	Organisation d'Armée Secrète (OAS) formed in Algeria
1964	Palestinian Liberation Organization (PLO) set up
1965	Suharto takes power in coup d'état in Indonesia
1967	George Habbash founds the Popular Front for the Liberation of Palestine (PFLP); first aeroplane hijacking July 1968

1968	Red Army Faction (also known as the Baader–Meinhof Gang) sets fire to department stores; officially formed as RAF in 1970; formally ended 1989
	Action for National Liberation (ALN) formed in Brazil; leader, Carlos Marighela, killed in 1969; defeated 1971
1969	August: PFLP hijacks TWA airliner on flight from Rome, Italy; forced to land in Damascus, Syria
1969–74	'Strategy of Tension' at its height in Italy; December 1969, bomb explodes in Piazza Fontana, Milan
1969	December: Provisional Irish Republican Army (PIRA) breaks away from the old IRA
1970	September: PFLP hijacks four airliners (two American, one Swiss, one British); one flown to Egypt, three to Dawson's Field, Jordan, where hostages held
	Black September formed by Abu Iyad, deputy leader of Al-Fatah
	Red Brigades (Brigate Rosse) forms in Italy; first victims in 1974; disbanded 1988
1971–79	Uganda under Idi Amin; mass killings and death squads
1972	Tutsi-dominated army massacres Hutus in Burundi
	May: members of the Japanese Red Army, with PFLP support, attack Lod airport in Israel, opening fire in the airport lounge

	21 July: PIRA sets off 22 bombs in Belfast, Northern Ireland
	September: Black September takes Israeli athletes hostage in Munich Olympic village, Germany
1973	Carlos the Jackal becomes the major PFLP organizer in Europe; January 1975, attacks an El Al airliner at Orly Airport, Paris, using an anti-tank rocket launcher
	Abu Nidal group first formed in Iraq; helps the Libyan-based group Arab Nationalist Youth Organization (ANYO) to hijack a KLM airliner
	September: Pinochet regime begins in Chile; ends 1989
1974	ETA splits into ETA-M and ETA-PM
	Abu Nidal sets up Fatah – the Revolutionary Council, with Iraqi sponsorship
1975–79	Terror Regime under the Khmer Rouge in Cambodia; Pol Pot prime minister of Democratic Kampuchea, April 1976
1975–99	State terrorism in East Timor, following invasion of Indonesian army
1975	December: PFLP attacks meeting, in Vienna, of the Organization of Petroleum Exporting Countries (OPEC)
1976–82	Argentina under military junta following March 1976 coup; Triple A death squad in operation
1976	June: Air France jet aeroplane hijacked at Athens Airport, Greece, by PFLP and RAF; forced to fly to Entebbe, Uganda

1976–78	Revolutionary Reign of Terror in Ethiopia; 'Red Terror' begins on 11 November 1977
1976	Tamil New Tigers, later changed to the Liberation Tigers of Tamil Eelan (LTTE), founded in Sri Lanka
1977	September: RAF and PFLP hijack Lufthansa airliner in Majorca; flown to Africa and landed in Mogadishu, Somalia
1979–84	Revolutionary Reign of Terror in Iran; Islamic Revolutionary Guard formed 5 March 1979
1980	May: Sendero Luminosa (the Shining Path) first uses terrorist tactics; leader Abimael Guzmán captured in September 1992
	August: right-wing bombing at Central Station, Bologna, Italy
	Islamic Jihad founded in Palestine
1980–92	State terrorism and death squads in El Salvador; Archbishop Romero killed 1980
1981–83	State terrorism in Guatemala under General Ríos Montt
1981	Khalistani Sikh terrorism begins in the Punjab, India; Bhindranwale killed in the Golden Temple in 1984; terrorism subsides from 1993
1982	Hizbollah created and sponsored by Iran in Lebanon
1983	April: Islamic Jihad suicide car bomb in Beirut
1984	April: Hizbollah bomb attack on a restaurant near Madrid, Spain

1984–85	December–January: peak of Euroterrorism that began in 1981
1985	June: Khalistani Sikh terrorists blow up an Air India airliner in flight over the Irish Sea, killing all passengers and crew
	September: Force 17 (Yasser Arafat's personal bodyguard) attacks and kills tourists on board a yacht in Cyprus
	October: Palestine Liberation Front (PLF) hijacks a passenger ship, *Achille Lauro*, on the coast of Egypt
	December: Abu Nidal group throw grenades and fire sub-machine guns at tourists queuing at El Al ticket counters at airports in Vienna and Rome
1986	April: La Belle Discotheque bombed in West Berlin by a Palestinian terrorist with help from East Germany and Libya
1987–89	Kurds killed in Iraq under Saddam Hussein; Kurdish uprising in 1991
1987	December: Hamas formed in West Bank and Gaza Strip
1988	December: terrorist bomb explodes on a Pan Am airliner over Lockerbie, Scotland, killing all on board; Libyan later sentenced
1991–95	'Ethnic cleansing' in Yugoslavia under Slobodan Milosovic; massacres in Bosnia, then Kosovo; the largest massacre in Srebrenica, 13–15 July 1995

1992	March: Hizbollah explode a car bomb in Buenos Aires, Argentina
1993	February: The Islamic Group, an Egyptian terrorist group, explodes a huge bomb in the World Trade Center, New York
1994	Rwanda: Genocidal campaign against the Tutsis led by the radical Hutu group 'Hutu Power'
	Carlos the Jackal captured in Sudan
	July: Iranian terrorist attack Jewish community centre in Buenos Aires, Argentina
1995	April: Oklahoma City bombing
	July: Algerian terrorist group, Armed Islamic Group (GIA), set off a bomb in a Paris underground station
1996	January: LTTE suicide bomber blows up Central Bank, Colombo, Sri Lanka
1998	August: al-Qaida carries out simultaneous car bomb attacks on the American embassies in Kenya and Tanzania
2001	September: '9/11', al-Qaida suicide bombers hijack four passenger aeroplanes and attack the Pentagon, Washington and the World Trade Center in New York
2002	October: Jemaah Islamiah (JI) explodes bomb in Bali, Indonesia, outside a bar and nightclub
2004	March: bombs left in rucksacks explode on commuter trains in Madrid, Spain; most likely al-Qaida
	September: Beslan, Russia: Chechen terrorists hold over 1,000 hostages in a school for three

days without water; large numbers of children are among the dead

2005 July: coordinated explosions on three underground trains and a bus carried out by suicide terrorists in London, England

September: Ismali Inqilabi Mahaz set off a series of explosions in a market in New Delhi, India

October: Jemaah Islamiah suicide bombers attack in Bali, Indonesia

November: Amman, Jordan, suicide terrorist attack on a hotel during a wedding reception

December: suicide bombing in shopping centre in Israel

December: suicide bomber blows up a passenger bus in Baghdad, Iraq

2006 January: suicide bomber kills pilgrims in Karbala, Iraq

March: al-Qaida blamed for attack on market in Sadr City in Baghdad, Iraq

March: series of bomb blasts in holy Hindu city in the state of Uttar Pradesh, India; Islamic militants blamed

April: car bomb explodes in a crowded street in Naraf, Iraq

April: suicide bomber outside a fast-food restaurant kills diners and passers-by in Tel Aviv, Israel; claimed by Islamic Jihad

April: series of bombs exploded in a restaurant, a café and a supermarket in the resort town of Dahab, Egypt

June: commuters and children on a bus killed by remotely detonated land mines in northern Sri Lanka; LTTE blamed

June: suicide bomber attacks a busy local market in Basra, Iraq

July: synchronized train bombings kill commuters in rush hour in Mumbai, India; Pakistan-based group Lashkar-e-Taiba blamed

August: wave of bomb blasts in Turkey; Kurdistan Freedom Falcons claim responsibility

August: homemade bombs exploded in a Moscow market

October: unarmed sailors going on leave killed by LTTE suicide bomber in Sri Lanka

December: Saddam Hussein hanged for crimes against humanity

December: after a nine-month ceasefire, ETA explodes a bomb inside a van at Madrid Airport

CHAPTER 1

Terrorism past and present

THE TERRORISM THAT HIT NEW YORK and Washington on 11 September 2001 had exactly the effects desired by all terrorists, past and present. Through terrible deeds the terrorists achieved a level of reaction and a creation of fear blown out of proportion to the reality of the size, efficiency and resources of the terrorist organization. On '9/11', these terrible deeds took the form of the hijacking of passenger aeroplanes full of innocent people, to be used as bombs by suicide terrorists. In New York, they successfully targeted the World Trade Center and caused the collapse of its twin towers, killing further innocent people. The final, official total of those killed, including members of the emergency rescue team, is 2,752 victims. It is the largest number of people ever killed in an act or coordinated set of acts carried out by a terrorist group on a single day.

In Washington, the aeroplane bomb hit the Pentagon, America's centre of defence. The President of the United States responded by declaring war on terrorism and, around the world,

In Washington, the aeroplane bomb hit the Pentagon, America's centre of defence. The President of the United States responded by declaring war on terrorism and, around the world, governments reacted by heightening their state's defences

governments reacted by heightening their state's defences. Since 2001, acts of terrorism have, nevertheless, continued. Among these incidents, one of the most shocking occurred almost exactly three years later. On 2–4 September 2004, in Beslan, Russia, Chechen terrorists held innocent schoolchildren, their parents and teachers, and even pre-school-age brothers and sisters captive in a school for three days without water: 1,128 hostages in total. At the end of the siege, the death toll was 330 people, more than half of them children. Earlier the same year, on 11 March 2004, ten bombs, left in rucksacks, exploded on commuter trains in Madrid, Spain, killing 19 people and injuring more than 1,400. In the following year, on 7 July 2005, coordinated explosions on three underground trains and a bus were carried out by suicide terrorists in London, England, killing 53 people and injuring another 750.

Two months later, in a series of explosions in New Delhi, India, 61 people died and a further 200 were injured in a market crowded with shoppers making purchases for the forthcoming Muslim and Hindu festivals. Only three days after, on 2 October 2005, suicide bombers killed a total of 44 people (including the bombers) and injured 100 people in Bali, Indonesia. The terrorist attack was organized by the same terrorist group, Jemaah Islamiah (JI), that had carried out bombings in Bali in October 2002 in which 202 people had been killed, most of them tourists gathered outside a bar and a nightclub. On 5 November 2005, a suicide terrorist attack was carried out on a hotel in Amman, Jordan: 57 people died and 93 were injured; 24 of the victims were members of a wedding party; both of the couple's fathers and the bride's mother were killed. On 5 December, five people were blown apart in a shopping centre in yet another suicide bombing in Israel. On 8 December, a suicide bomber blew up a bus as it left a bus station in Baghdad, Iraq, killing 30 people. Four months before, in August, 43 people had been killed and 89 injured in a similar incident. Within days of the start of 2006, a suicide bomber killed 60 pilgrims in Karbala, Iraq.

The year 2006 continued as it had begun. In Iraq, further terrorist incidents occurred, each killing between 10 and 58 people: in a Baghdad market in March, a crowded street in Naraf in April, and a market in Basra in June. In August, ten people were killed when homemade bombs exploded in a market in Moscow. Restaurants too were attacked: in April, a suicide bomber blew up a fast-food restaurant in Tel Aviv, Israel, killing 9 people and injuring 50 others; in August, in the resort town of Dahab in Egypt, bombs exploded in a restaurant, a café and a supermarket, killing at least 30 people. Also in August, a wave of bomb blasts in tourist areas in Turkey killed 3 people and injured more than 30. In Sri Lanka, in June, 64 people were killed, at least 15 of them children, when land mines suspended from trees were detonated above a bus by remote control; the attack was blamed on the Tamil Tigers. In October, a Tamil Tiger suicide bomber killed 93 sailors and wounded 150 more; the sailors were unarmed and going on leave. In India, in March, a series of bomb blasts, blamed on Islamic militants, hit the holy Hindu city of Varanasi in the state of Uttar Pradesh, killing 15 people and injuring at least four times as many. India also experienced the worst of all the incidents that occurred in 2006. In July, 207 people were killed and a further 700 injured in synchronized train bombings carried out in the rush hour in Mumbai; a Sunni Islamic group, Lashkar-e-Taiba, has been blamed.

These terrible deeds brought the terrorists immediate and wide publicity. Through the means of modern communications technology, news and pictures of the events were quickly circulated around the globe. All these acts of terrorism produced widespread shock and fear of future such events, and in the case of '9/11' the shock and fear were heightened through the very audacity of the enterprise and the spectacular nature of the outcome. The drama of the planes crashing into the towers was then followed by their breathtaking collapse. The spectacular nature of '9/11' ensured not only widespread publicity but also that the story and its pictures would stay in the public eye. Added to this, the terrorists achieved another goal: there was reaction resulting not only from shock and fear but also from admiration of both the spectacle and the demonstration of the vulnerability of a super power, the United States. So, support was strengthened among the terrorists' sympathizers and the size of their pool of supporters expanded. The events in Madrid in 2004 and, more tentatively, those in London in 2005 have been linked to al-Qaida, the terrorist group that carried out the attacks in New York and Washington on 11 September 2001.

The terrorism of '9/11' employed the advantages of modern technology: aeroplanes, satellite phones, televisions and a host of related devices and infrastructures. The strategy employed by the terrorists also exploited the nature of modern society. Urbanization with its high population density and high-rise buildings has produced conditions that maximize the impact of terrorist acts. A bomb carried by just one person can achieve a huge impact: damage to property bringing serious disruption and, far worse, the deaths and injuries of large numbers of innocent people. Large buildings full of people living, working, studying, being educated or entertained are efficient targets for terrorist attacks. Public transport networks similarly draw together large numbers of people and the damage caused by explosions accentuates the disruption. Furthermore, as well as modern transport and communications networks facilitating dramatic terrorist acts, they also enable the communication and organization of the terrorist group itself.

Terrorist groups are cloaked in secrecy and the clandestine nature of their operations and their underground organizations are aided not only by the speed and accessibility of modern communications and transport but also by the anonymity of modern city life. Ironically, too, for it stands in such contrast to the secrecy of terrorist organizations, the interests of terrorist groups are also served by the openness of modern, democratic society. Freedom of information enables the more effective planning of terrorist acts. Freedom of association can also be exploited as a cover for terrorist groups and innocent organizations and associations can be infiltrated not only as cover but also for the

Terrorist groups are cloaked in secrecy and the clandestine nature of their operations and their underground organizations are aided not only by the speed and accessibility of modern communications and transport but also by the anonymity of modern city life

purpose of generating recruits. Freedom of the press and other media also ensures that acts of terrorism gain wide publicity. In a closed society there would be no such access to information or freedom of movement and association and no such publicity for terrorist acts.

Although the events of 11 September 2001 were dramatically modern in their use of technology and their exploitation of urbanization and the open society, the identification of the Islamic terrorist group al-Qaida as the perpetrators has highlighted a connection that is far from modern: that between terrorist groups and religion. Indeed, it is a connection that has a history stretching back to the earliest examples of terrorist groups.

Early terrorist groups: holy terror

Nearly two millennia ago, in Ancient Palestine, the Zealots-Sicarii used terrorism as a means to oppose the Roman occupation of Judea. At the time, Josephus Flavius, a Jewish commander who changed to become a Roman supporter and historian, records how the Zealots-Sicarii mingled in the crowds in Jerusalem committing murders using the short daggers (sica) that they had concealed in their clothes. Josephus also records how they avoided detection by convincingly joining in with the crowd as they reacted with cries of shock. Such murders occurred on a daily pattern:

The panic created was more alarming than the calamity itself; everyone, as on the battlefield, hourly expected death. Men kept watch at a distance on their enemies and would not trust even their friends when they approached.

(Josephus Flavius, quoted in Rapoport, 1984: 670)

The aim of the Zealots-Sicarii was to undermine political authority, including not only Roman but also Jewish political authority, in order to provoke hatred between Jews, Romans and Greeks and so to completely destroy politics as a possible solution. The objective was mass uprising as the passage to Messianic deliverance. The mass revolt was achieved between 66 and 70 AD; the end was failure and mass suicide at Masada in 73 AD.

'Zealot' is a term still used today and is sometimes applied to modern terrorists. The words 'assassin' and 'thug' are also used and they, too, have their origins in early examples of terrorism. Zealots-Sicarii, Thugs and Assassins – Jews, Hindus and Muslims, respectively – all engaged in holy terror

'Zealot' is a term still used today and is sometimes applied to modern terrorists. The words 'assassin' and 'thug' are also used and they, too, have their origins in early examples of terrorism

(Rapoport, 1984). The Assassins, strictly members of the Ismaili branch of Shia Islam, were active during the years 1090–1275, and they operated in crowded places using daggers. Unlike the Zealots-Sicarii, who adopted tactics for avoiding detection in order to repeat their terrorist act another day, the Assassins aimed to carry out just one act: their own death to be a means to publicize their mission. Those carrying out the acts, the *fedayeen*, sought martyrdom in order to reach paradise. In Shia Islam, religious and political objectives are combined in the mission to fulfil Islam in its pure form. Designed for maximum impact in both their highly public nature and the martyrdom that followed, the assassinations had the effect of threatening governments, especially of those states, within the then Turkish Seljuk Empire, in regions of today's Iran and Syria.

The Thugs of India lasted by far the longest. Probably around in the seventh century AD, they were at their height in the thirteenth century and continued for perhaps as long as a further six centuries. Unlike the Zealots-Sicarii and the Assassins, the Thugs killed not in crowded places using daggers but in isolated areas and they murdered travellers by strangulation and then dissected the bodies, so violating Hindu burial rites. The Thugs' purpose was purely religious: their goal was to please the Goddess Kali, the goddess of terror and destruction. Temporally the closest of the three to modern times, in lacking a political goal the Thugs are the most distant from modern terrorist groups. Their importance in the history of terrorism is found in the extreme fear that they produced in the wider population and in the vast numbers of people who died at their hands, over so long a time. The Thugs also prefigured an aspect of modern terrorist organization in their clearly laid down code of rules. These covered such things as training, conduct, restrictions on kinds of victim, the number of killings required of each assassin and the division of labour.

Today, examples similar to Zealots, Assassins and Thugs are to be found not only in al-Qaida, which carried out the attacks in New York and Washington on 11 September 2001, but also in Jemaah Islamiah, which carried out the Bali bombings in 2002 and 2005, and in Ismali Inqilabi Mahaz, which carried out the attack in New Delhi in 2005. As Muslim groups, they have similarities with the Assassins but are far from being the only such examples: two cases covered in later chapters are the Palestinian groups Islamic Jihad and Hamas. Modern-day examples similar to the Zealots can also be found in the Middle East: the young Jewish extremist Yigal Amir who assassinated the Prime Minister of Israel, Yitzak Rabin, in November 1995 has obvious similarities, as too does the Stern Gang, the extremist Zionist group founded in 1940. In India, the Khalistani Sikh terrorist groups of the Punjab, active from the 1980s, are a modern-day equivalent of the Thugs: the Sikh religion broke from the Hindu religion in the seventeen century. One other striking example for not having Jewish, Muslim or Hindu connections is that of the followers of the Aum Shinri-Ky sect, a Japanese Buddhist sect, which perpetrated the nerve gas attack on the Tokyo subway in March 1995.

Although the Zealots, the Assassins and the Thugs show that the existence of terrorism in the form of terrorist groups has a long history, the term 'terrorism' itself did not enter the English language until the final decade of the eighteenth century. Furthermore, it did so not through the acts of terrorist groups attacking government but through the conduct

Although the Zealots, the Assassins and the Thugs show that the existence of terrorism in the form of terrorist groups has a long history, the term 'terrorism' itself did not enter the English language until the final decade of the eighteenth century

of a regime. As first conceived, terrorism meant 'system of terror', the term formed from the Latin word 'terror', which in Roman times meant physical trembling. 'Terrorism' was coined to condemn the rule of the Jacobins in the French Revolution.

The Reign of Terror in the French Revolution

In the short space of 17 months between the spring of 1793 and the high summer of 1794 the revolutionary regime in France carried out 17,000 official executions. The Jacobins, the radical revolutionaries, gained control over the National Convention in March 1793. Their rule became known as the Reign of Terror. They lasted in power until the end of July 1794, their fall marked by Maximilien Robespierre, the head of the Committee of Public Safety, being sent to the guillotine.

Maximilien Robespierre, 1758–94

Born in Arras in 1758, Robespierre became a barrister in 1781. In March 1789 he was elected to the Estates-General, which had not met since 1614. After the revolution of 14 July 1789, Robespierre distinguished himself in debates in the National Assembly. A radical, primarily influenced by the works of Jean-Jacques Rousseau, he was a member of the Breton Club, later to be known as the Jacobins after the monastery in which the club met. The Committee of Public Safety was decreed in April 1793 and in July Robespierre was elected to be one of its 12 members. He gained popular support as 'the Incorruptible'. In the last three months of Jacobin rule, after those most in favour of terror, Hébert's group – the Héberistes – and those most opposed, Danton and supporters – the Indulgents – were guillotined, Robespierre effectively ruled supreme. In June he inaugurated the festival of the Supreme Being, a state religion to replace Catholicism. He, along with 21 of his close allies, was arrested on the night of 27–28 July 1794 and sent to the guillotine: 9–10 Thermidor in the new revolutionary calendar. It is from this date that the end of the Reign of Terror gets its name – Thermidor.

The vast majority of the official executions were carried out without proper trials to establish guilt; suspicion, not hard evidence, became sufficient grounds for arrest. In addition to the official executions, more than half a million people were held prisoner, with old ships and warehouses being used as makeshift prisons. The effects of crowded conditions and disease among these prisoners took a further toll; many of those prisoners died of disease before they came to trial. Captured rebels (mainly from the west of France) were shot or drowned without ever being sent for trial. In total, the toll of the Terror is estimated to have been between 35,000 and 40,000 people (Greer, 1966).

Varieties of regime terrorism

Rulers terrorized their subjects long before the the Jacobins began terrorizing French citizens. Emperors such as Nero, Justinian II and Ghengis Khan were infamous even in their own time. The Reign of Terror in France is distinguished from these earlier regimes because the revolution was supposed to be modern, enlightened and rational. By 1789, the era of modern thinking had already begun. Ideas of government by

Rulers terrorized their subjects long before the Jacobins began terrorizing French citizens. Emperors such as Nero, Justinian II and Ghengis Khan were infamous even in their own time

consent and trials based on reason were already the practice in Britain and America. In modern, enlightened thinking, torture, used as the state's method for extracting evidence, as it had been throughout medieval times, was no longer considered acceptable practice.

After the French Revolution, however, regimes of terror have continued. The terrors in the Russian, Ethiopian and Iranian revolutions stand out. They will be expanded on in Chapter 3. Appalling cases of terror governments have also occurred outside of revolution. The two most shocking have been so not only because of the numbers of victims involved and the horrors that took place but also because they harnessed the very science and technology of enlightenment and happened seemingly in the very midst of twentieth-century democracies. These terror regimes occurred in the Soviet Union under Stalin and in Germany under Hitler, with Germany actually a democracy before its destruction by the Nazi regime.

As an indication of the scale of the horrors in the Soviet Union, estimates for the number of people who died as a consequence of the collectivization programme, 1929–35, range between 2.5 million and 10.5 million; current estimates of deaths under the Great Purges, 1936–38, range between one and three million. In Germany, from Hitler's rise to power in 1933 to the end of Nazi rule in 1945, close to six million Jews were killed, as well as tens of thousands of Gypsies, mentally ill people, physically incurable people, homosexuals and Jehovah's Witnesses. As in Stalin's Soviet Union, many more victims were also worked to death or died in transit. In Cambodia under Pol Pot, an estimated one million people were killed as a direct consequence of Khmer Rouge policies: approximately one-seventh of the population. In the genocidal campaign carried out in Rwanda in 1994 around half a million people out of a population of eight million were butchered to death. And these are only some of the cases that will be expanded on in chapters to come.

The people killed by any one of these regimes of terror far outnumber those killed by any one terrorist group or terrorist network. The single exception is the Thugs; just in the last three centuries of their existence, the seventeenth to nineteenth, they probably killed around 500,000 victims, the high total being partly the consequence of the extraordinary length of time that they existed (Rapoport, 1984). Given the enormity of the crimes committed by terror regimes, it seems odd, therefore, that terrorism today usually conjures up the image not of terror regime but of terrorist group. Especially odd, given that the word, terrorism, was first coined to apply to a regime. To some extent the sheer proliferation of terrorist groups helps to explain this image of terrorism, but it is also to do with the differences between the kinds of society in which these two forms of terrorism occur.

By their nature terror regimes take place in closed societies, the outside world not learning the extent of the horrors until the regime falls. Evidence of current acts of terrorism leaks out and is then challenged by the regime. In

> *By their nature terror regimes take place in closed societies, the outside world not learning the extent of the horrors until the regime falls*

contrast, the acts of terrorism perpetrated by terrorist groups are associated with more open societies. Publicity, as will become clear, is a crucial aspect of terrorist group strategy and reporting of terrorist acts in the media is essential to their impact. Hearing and reading so much about them and seeing the drama and devastation in pictures and on screen, it is not so surprising that the association between terrorism and terrorist groups is uppermost in the minds of those privileged to live in open societies. This link is then reinforced through the open discussion and speculation that such societies allow.

Terrorist groups today, as the example of '9/11' has so clearly illustrated, exploit modern open society, with its freedoms of information and association, exploit modern science and technology, and take advantage of modern urbanization. Unlike al-Qaida, however, modern terrorist groups first entered the history books as decidedly secular organizations.

Modern terrorism: anarchists to left-wing terrorist groups

The invention of dynamite in 1862 and its development into gelignite in 1875 opened the way for modern terrorism. No longer was it necessary for assassins to make direct attacks on individuals: now explosives could be left in public places or thrown into crowds. With the door thus opened, the step into modern terrorism was taken with a new political idea and a new slogan: 'propaganda by the deed'. The idea of 'propaganda by the deed' was first advocated by the delegates of the Italian Federation at the Anarchist International held in December 1876. In their declaration it was proposed as the means towards a political end, the anarchists' interpretation of socialism. The idea behind the slogan was that dramatic action, for example the explosion of a bomb to assassinate a top political figure, spoke louder than words and could rally support more effectively and demonstrate, at one and the same time, both the true nature of repressive government and its vulnerability to being overthrown.

The Russian anarchist Peter Kropotkin set out the theory, as follows:

One such act may, in a few days, make more propaganda than a thousand pamphlets. Above all, it awakens the spirit of revolt; it breeds daring. . . . Soon it becomes apparent that the established order does not have the strength often supposed. One courageous act has sufficed to upset in a few days the entire governmental machinery . . .
(Peter Kropotkin, quoted in Iviansky, 1977: 45)

Kropotkin elaborates on how the savagery of the government's retaliation would reveal the true, repressive nature of the government and how the vulnerability of the state machinery would be demonstrated through the government's being so

---

Peter Kropotkin, 1842–1921

Born in Moscow into an aristocratic family, Princes of Smolensk descended from the Grand Prince of Kiev, Prince Piotr Alekseyevich Kropotkin became an officer in Tsar Nicholas I's army. He left the army to become a geographer and then became an anarchist joining the International, in Switzerland, in 1872. He returned to Russia to begin undercover propaganda. Arrested in 1874 and imprisoned, he escaped the same year and left Russia, not to return until after the 1917 Revolution. While in France he was the founding editor of *Le Révolté* until imprisoned there, too, in 1882. Concerted protests by writers and academics and, not least, scientists because he had published important scientific works led to his release in 1885. He left for England, where he stayed for over 30 years and where he wrote his major books, including *Mutual Aid* (1902), in which he extols the importance of cooperation. On his return to Russia he became disillusioned with the Bolshevik government and dedicated his time to writing.

---

easily shaken by so small a thing as a terrorist's bomb. In theory, the effect would be to encourage further revolts, both as individual acts of terrorism and as mass insurrection. Like that of the Zealots-Sicarii, the aim was to achieve the total destabilization of the regime.

A bomb is inherently less discriminating in its target than is the use of a dagger, a noose or, for that matter, a revolver. With the use of a bomb, innocent bystanders run a high risk of being killed or injured. Bombs, especially when fitted with timing devices, may also hinder detection of the perpetrator by enabling his or her escape. Both the nature of the chaos caused by the explosion and the heightened problem of finding the terrorist and stopping the terrorism through rooting out the terrorist organization adds to the image of ineffectual government, even as state repression is being increased. As Morozov, member of the Russian populist group Land and Liberty (*Zemla i Volya*), wrote in the *Bulletin of the Land and Liberty* in March 1879:

the blow at the very centre of government organization . . . will transmit itself, as an electric current, throughout the entire state and will cause disruption and confusion in all its activities.
(Nicholas Morozov, quoted in Ivianski, 2001: 135)

Disagreements in *Land and Liberty* over Morozov's advocacy of political assassination as the means for revolution, together with an attempt made on the Tsar's life in April 1879, led to the setting up of the People's Will (*Narodnaya Volya*).

The People's Will was the first modern terrorist organization. What made the group different from the earlier anarchist groups was its underground organization. Instead of each assassination being carried out on the initiative of an extremist individual, the

People's Will planned and organized terrorist acts for the grand political purpose of overthrowing the regime. In 1881 it succeeded in assassinating Tsar Alexander II. Although the assassination failed to lead to the mass uprising the group had expected, it succeeded in

The People's Will was the first modern terrorist organization. What made the group different from the earlier anarchist groups was its underground organization

pushing the state into severely repressive acts. The effect was to greatly weaken the group. In 1887, with most of the leaders captured and many executed, the People's Will set out to repeat its 'blow at the very centre of government', but this time the plot to assassinate Tsar Alexander III was foiled and the plotters were arrested and executed.

The People's Will advocated terrorism as the means to revolution in Russia because Russia was an autocracy reliant on a highly coercive state. The group did not advocate terrorism in parliamentary regimes, where opposition was both legal and real. The reasoning behind this view was that in repressive regimes terrorist tactics could be justified as an efficient means for destabilizing government because it would save the lives of those who would otherwise be slaughtered in mass revolution. Peasants, they argued, would be far more vulnerable to state onslaught than workers living in towns and cities who could be more effectively organized for fighting behind barricades. Outside Russia, however, contrasting with the logic of the People's Will, terrorist activity was taking place not only in repressive countries but also in those with democratic institutions that guaranteed legal opposition, including competing political parties.

Emile Henry

The 1890s became known as 'the decade of the bomb' and terrorist attacks were especially frequent in Paris, including the bomb set off by the anarchist August Vaillant in the Chamber of Deputies in 1893. A week after the execution of Vaillant, in 1894, the anarchist Emile Henry exploded a bomb in a crowded café, the Café Terminus, near the St Lazarre railway station, in Paris, killing one person and injuring 19 others. At his trial, in his defence for exploding a bomb where ordinary members of the public were innocently sitting at tables and café employees were carrying out their daily work, Henry reflected on an earlier bomb that he had left at the door of the building where the Carmaux Company had its offices:

What about the innocent victims? I soon resolved that question. The building where the Carmaux Company had its offices was inhabited only by bourgeois: hence there would be no innocent victims.
(Emile Henry, *Gazette des Tribunaux*, 27–28 April 1894, translated in Woodcock, 1977: 193)

Expanding on all those included under the term 'bourgeois' and referring specifically to the Café Terminus bomb, Henry adds to those 'who live idly on the profits of the worker's toil' (p. 195):

And not only they, but all those who are satisfied with the existing order . . . that stupid and pretentious mass of folk who always choose the strongest side – in other words, the daily clientele of Terminus and the other great cafés!
(p. 195)

In Henry's logic the café, frequented by bourgeoisie, was a justifiable target because the place was representative of the class as a whole and, therefore, of the entire political and economic order and, indeed, all that was corrupt and wrong with society. This was why there were 'no innocent victims'.

While anarchists justified their use of terrorism against liberal democratic governments in terms similar to those of Henry and the People's Will argued for terrorist tactics only to be used against repressive regimes, like autocratic Russia, terrorist tactics were roundly rejected by Marxist groups. In line with all Social Democratic parties, the Russian Social Democratic Party, which was set up in 1883 and which split into the Menshevik and Bolshevik parties in 1903, rejected *Narodnaya Volya*'s terrorist strategy. Although the successful assassination of Tsar Alexander II was admired, Social Democratic parties, as Marxist parties, supported proletarian revolution based on strikes, demonstrations, barricades and fighting concentrated in urban areas.

In 1901–02, however, the terrorist strategy of the People's Will was revived when a new party, the Russian Socialist Revolutionary Party (SR), was created by a group that included former members of the People's Will. The Socialist Revolutionary Party adopted both the rural emphasis and the terrorist strategy advocated by the People's Will and created the SR Combat Organization for the purpose. In 1908, though, the use of terror was rejected by the party when leading advocate and practitioner, Azev, was exposed as a double agent, destroying the image of terrorists as those willing to risk their lives for the betterment of all. Although at first siding with the Bolsheviks in the Russian Revolution of 1917, following the Bolshevik government's signing of a peace treaty with Germany in March 1918, the

Brest–Litovsk Treaty, terrorist groups once again split from the Socialist Revolutionaries. This time they turned their assassination attacks on Bolsheviks in their attempt to bring down Lenin's new government. As we know, they failed and the Soviet Union remained under Communist Party government until 1991.

In the twentieth century, new left-wing groups emerged that brought together ideas and strategies in combinations that, in the nineteenth century, had been rejected by both activists and theorists

In the twentieth century, new left-wing groups emerged that brought together ideas and strategies in combinations that, in the nineteenth century, had been rejected by both activists and theorists. Ideas inspired by Marxism, which originally argued for a Communist Party and proletarian revolution based on strikes, demonstrations and barricades in urban areas, were combined with terrorist strategy and tactics. Contrary to the position taken by the People's Will, furthermore, their acts of terrorism were carried out within liberal democracies. In more recent times the most notable examples of these new left-wing terrorist groups are the Red Army Faction (Rote Armée Fraktion, also known as the Baader–Meinhof Gang), which formed in Germany in 1968, and the Red Brigades (Brigate Rosse), which formed in Italy in 1970. These will be a focus of Chapter 6.

The new Marxist-inspired ideas developed, in part at least, in consequence of the unanticipated events of intervening history. The most important of these events were the Nazi regime in Germany and the fascist regime in Italy, which were ended in 1945. Other significant occurrences were the revolutions through Communist Party guerrilla armies in China and Vietnam and a non-party 'foco' guerrilla movement in Cuba. In the developing world, the most notorious left-wing terrorist group, which will be covered in some detail in Chapter 7, was the Shining Path (Sendero Luminosa), which formed in Peru and combined Maoist with nationalist ideas.

Terrorist groups and varieties of nationalism

Nationalism is a crucial motivation for many twentieth-century terrorist groups and, not least, that of the terrorist group with the longest history in modern times: the Irish Republican Army/ Provisional IRA (IRA/PIRA). The outbreak of the First World War led to the suspension in the British Parliament of the new Home Rule Bill for Ireland. The resulting Easter Rising in Dublin, in 1916, and its failure led to the formation of the IRA as a nationalist organization committed to the use of force to further its aim of freeing Ireland from British rule. Following the partition of Ireland in 1922, which left the six counties of Northern Ireland under British government, the IRA continued a violent campaign both against British rule in the North and against the Irish government of the South for rejecting violence as the means to achieve a united Ireland. This, too, is a case that will be expanded on in Chapter 6; other cases mentioned below will also feature in detail in chapters to come.

Nationalism is multifaceted. The aim of independence in com-bination with the protection of language and culture is found in the two other best-known, enduring terrorist groups. In the Basque region of Spain, *Euskadi 'ta Askatasuna* (Basque Homeland and Freedom, ETA), formed in 1959 with the declared aims of

Basque independence and promotion of the Basque language and culture. In 1976, a similar terrorist group formed seeking homeland (Eelam) and based on an ethnic minority (the Tamils) concentrated in the north of Sri Lanka: the Liberation Tigers of Tamil Eelam (LTTE). In the 1980s this group introduced suicide terrorist attacks for the first time since the Assassins of so long ago.

Anti-colonialism is another facet of nationalism and some of these movements, though far from all, have engaged in terrorist violence. The most famous case is the Algerian National Liberation Front (FLN), which ran a bombing campaign in Algiers from 1956 to 1962, the year in which independence was finally gained and the French colonial government departed from Algeria. Groups within the Palestine Liberation Organization (PLO), such as al-Fatah and the Popular Front for the Liberation of Palestine (PFLP), have similarly used terrorism to further their nationalist goals. The case of the Armed Forces for Liberation (FALN), which formed in Puerto Rico in 1974, also deserves mention as an unusual case. Although Puerto Rico has been an associated free state of the United States since 1952, nationalist anti-US sentiments led FALN to explode bombs in New York, Chicago, San Francisco and Washington, DC. In the most famous incident, the explosion of a bomb in the historic Fraunce's Tavern in New York in 1975, 4 people were killed and 45 others injured.

Nationalism has yet one more facet that is found in terrorist groups: these terrorists target not the government but groups within society that are viewed, in their eyes, as threatening the status quo. With white supremacy at its heart, the Ku Klux Klan is a glaring example; it originated in the United States following the defeat of the Confederates, the supporters of slavery, in the Civil War of 1861–65. Initially the Ku Klux Klan directed its terror against African-Americans with the aim of 'keeping them in their place'. Over time, the target groups expanded to Jews, Catholics and communists,

Nationalism has yet one more facet that is found in terrorist groups: these terrorists target not the government but groups within society that are viewed, in their eyes, as threatening the status quo

indeed anyone viewed as not representing '100 per cent Americanism' (Sprinzak, 1995: 32).

Such nationalist, racist, anti-Semitic and anti-communist ideas drew not only on America's history but also on European events and ideas. After the First World War, in part as reaction to the peace settlements, two new political movements developed, each spawning new ideologies: Fascism in Italy and National Socialism in Germany. Both these ideologies were nationalist, anti-communist, anti-socialist and anti-liberal; National Socialism, Nazism, was also anti-Semitic and racist. Although both Mussolini's Fascist state and Hitler's Nazi regime were defeated in the Second World War, their examples have served as imagery for modern right-wing terrorist groups, fascist and racist alike. In Europe, notable examples include the neo-Nazis in Germany, *Deutsche Aktionsgruppe*, and the neo-fascists in Italy, *Nuclei Armati Rivoluzionari*, both of which formed in 1980. The targets of such groups have included synagogues, foreign workers and hostels for asylum seekers. The imagery of ZOG (Zionist Occupation Government) has also developed to tarnish governments considered too liberal. First conceived in the United States in the late 1970s, the idea of ZOG has since spread to other extreme-right groups beyond America.

International terrorism

Not only ideas travel. Just as the invention of gelignite enabled the idea of 'propaganda by the deed' to explode into practice, so innovations in modern communication and transport enabled the development of international terrorism. Acts such as hijacking passenger airliners, flying the hostages to foreign countries and negotiating with foreign governments are the essence of international terrorism. As an illustration, one of the most dramatic examples occurred in June 1976: an Air France airliner was hijacked at Athens Airport, Greece, forced to fly to Libya for refuelling and then on to Entebbe, Uganda. Once arrived in Entebbe, with the support of the president of Uganda, Idi Amin, the crew and passengers were held hostage and negotiations were entered into involving a number of foreign governments for the release of 53 terrorists held in gaols in various countries, including Germany. The outcome involved Israel's anti-terror squad storming the hijacked plane, in Entebbe. Without modern technology, not least the jet aeroplane, telephone network and modern media technology, none of this could have taken place; without the means for achieving global publicity, such dramatic acts on an international scale would be pointless. As this example also demonstrates, for it involved both the Popular Front for the Liberation of Palestine (PFLP) and the German Red Army Faction (RAF), modern technologies also eased the way for cooperation between terrorist groups across and beyond countries' borders.

With the idea of 'propaganda by the deed' being so absolutely central to the terrorism of terrorist groups it is not surprising that advances in modern media technology have been accompanied, in recent years, by a growth in the number of both terrorist acts and terrorist groups. Terrorism can so easily be viewed as the 'quick fix' cure-all solution, especially for groups that lack size, efficiency and resources in their organization. To claim that terrorist groups have grown in number over time requires, however, a concept of terrorism capable of separating out real cases from events staged simply to seek publicity. To be of value, such a concept should also be able to identify the characteristics of terrorism common both to terrorist groups and to terror regimes. With this background on terrorism past and present it is time, therefore, to turn more directly to the concept of terrorism.

Recommended reading

For readings on anarchist terrorist groups, George Woodcock, ed., *The Anarchist Reader* (Glasgow: Fontana/Collins, 1977) is the crucial work. For a discussion of modern terrorism, the chapters by Zeev Ivianski, 'The Terrorist Revolution: Roots of Modern Terrorism', in David C. Rapoport, ed., *Inside Terrorist Organizations* (London: Frank Cass, 2001), and by Philip Pomper, 'Russian Revolutionary Terrorism', in Martha Crenshaw, ed., *Terrorism in Context* (Pennsylvania: The Pennsylvania State University Press, 1995) are excellent. The classic work on the Jacobin reign of terror is Donald Greer, *The Incidence of the Terror during the French Revolution: A Statistical Interpretation* (Gloucester, MA.: Peter Smith, 1966). This and other revolutionary reigns of terror are covered in detail in Chapter 3. Similarly, expansion on Nazi Germany, Stalin's Soviet Union and Cambodia under Pol Pot is found in Chapter 4 and on Rwanda in Chapter 5.

The modern terrorist groups introduced as examples will be covered in detail along with recommended reading in later chapters: the IRA, RAF, Red Brigades and ETA in Chapter 6; the Tamil Tigers, the Shining Path, the Khalistani Sikh groups, the FLN, the Stern Gang and the PLO in Chapter 7; the PFLP, Islamic Jihad, Hamas and al-Qaida in Chapter 8, which also includes further coverage of the PLO groups. The FLN also features in Chapter 2. More on right-wing terrorism is to be found in Chapters 5 and 6.

Keesing's Contemporary Archives to 1987 (London and Harlow: Keesing's Publications, Longman), re-named *Keesing's Record of World Events* from 1988 (Cambridge Keesing's Worldwide), are excellent primary sources for all recent examples of terrorism. A valuable secondary source, which also includes earlier cases, is Martha Crenshaw and John Pimlott, eds, *Encyclopedia of World Terrorism*, vols. I–III (Armonk: NY: M.E. Sharpe, 1997).

CHAPTER 2

The concept of terrorism

WHEN GEORGE BUSH DECLARED 'war' on 'terrorism' in the aftermath of '9/11' it fell into line with Cold War imagery of the fight against communism: the victory claimed after the fall of the Berlin Wall and then the disintegration of the Soviet Union. The 'isms' of fascism and Nazism, too, had been fought and destroyed in the Second World War. But terrorism – political terrorism, that is – is not like other 'isms'.

Terrorism is not a political ideology. Nazism, communism, fascism, socialism, anarchism, liberalism and

Terrorism is not a political ideology

conservatism logically imply distinctive sets of ideas. To be an ideology, the set of ideas should involve critical assessment of other political ideas and realities together with alternative proposals on a preferred political system and society and those ideas should also impact significantly on the actions of those who believe in them. The crucial ideas behind terrorism, however, relate to the justification for the use of terror as a strategy, the use of violence to engender fear for those political ends. Terrorism, therefore, may be found alongside any political ideology that does not contain a rejection of the use of violence in its own set of ideas. This is why neither terrorist groups nor terror regimes are associated exclusively with either left-wing or right-wing thinking, and terrorism may also be associated, as in the holy terror of the Thugs, Zealots and Assassins, with ideas that fit comfortably with neither left nor right descriptions.

That political terrorism has a basic belief in the justification for the use of violence for political ends, its purpose to produce fear in order to achieve political goals, is a common theme in the literature on the concept of terrorism. It does not, however, amount to a definition of terrorism: this is because the fear produced by the use of violence may be of two kinds. The distinction between these two kinds of fear hinges on whether or not the violence is arbitrary, that is, used indiscriminately against guilty and innocent alike.

Violence against innocents

The importance of the distinction between the use of violence against the guilty and its use against innocents was made by one of the principal Italian fascist thinkers, Sergio Panunzio (Gregor, 1982). Panunzio used it to justify attacks on communists and socialists in the situation of 'internal war' that characterized the fascists' rise to power in Italy. For fascists, communists and socialists were enemies, their guilt demonstrated by their own chosen behaviour of supporting the communist and socialist parties; as such, violence could be justified in its use against them. What Panunzio argued could not be justified was the use of violence against the innocent. The deliberate use of violence against innocent victims as a means to an end, including the generation of fear in others, he classified as terror.

Even allowing for the brutality of the violence used by fascists in practice, Panunzio's emphasis on the arbitrary indiscriminate nature of terror and its focus on innocent victims is crucial to the concept of terrorism. Knowing what acts they were not allowed to do, communists and socialists could change their behaviour (to the compliant behaviour of no longer opposing fascism) and so avoid the violence meted out by the fascists. The purpose of the violence was intimidation: designed not only to punish the 'guilty' but also to serve as a warning to those who might also engage in proscribed behaviour. Intimidation is not the same as terrorism.

Violence used to force people into compliant behaviour makes clear what behaviour is proscribed. Those who engage in the proscribed behaviour are punished so that others will be intimidated

Violence used to force people into compliant behaviour makes clear what behaviour is proscribed

through fear of similar punishment into changing their actual or intended behaviour. Terrorism, however, does not aim to intimidate with the objective of changing people's behaviour to compliance. Terrorism, which arbitrarily targets both the guilty and innocent alike, produces not the fear that follows from intimidation but the terror that comes from the unknown, over which there is no means of control. Terrorism neither makes clear the behaviour that is proscribed nor sets down precisely the behaviours with which to comply: the victimization of innocents is deliberate.

A simple example helps to demonstrate this crucial aspect of terror that follows from the deliberate victimization of innocents. I use it with my students. In the seminar I choose an item of clothing, blue jeans or brown shoes, perhaps, and select those wearing the item and reprimand them, threatening punishment, and proclaim that they or anyone who comes to next week's seminar wearing such items will be severely punished. (Taken outside and shot is the usual threat made, supported by the claim that I have a gun in my pocket. If my threat is not believed, which it mostly is not, I quickly change my threat to that of having essay marks reduced.) I then ask both the picked-on members of the group and the group as a whole what they expect themselves and others to do. After suitable banter about not believing that I would carry out even my weaker threat of reducing essay marks, their agreed reply is always that next week they will not be wearing blue jeans or brown shoes. The intimidation has worked.

In the next step in my demonstration of the difference between the fear produced by intimidation and the fear produced by terror, I then pick on someone else, at random, and, pointing my concealed gun, declare that I have shot them. I then ask the others what they will do, what action they will take to avoid being the next victim. Is it the colour of their trousers or their shoes? Their answer, of course, is that they do not know; they cannot know what behaviour to change. The best they can suggest is that they will adopt no action, will seek to avoid attention. In reality, there is nothing that they can do to reduce their chances of indiscriminate punishment. The person picked on was not guilty of any known proscribed behaviour and neither had the victim been sentenced in error. The victim was chosen arbitrarily: an innocent.

Regimes of terror

In the Reign of Terror of 1793–94, which took place during the French Revolution under Robespierre and the Committees of Public Safety and of General Security, fear was produced by unpredictability, the arbitrary use of violence. This kind of fear – terror – was epitomized by the sudden arrival of the people's armies, 'the terror on the move' (Cobb, 1987: 2), lashing out in 'blind violence and sometimes cruelty' (p. 512). It was also present in the operation of the surveillance committees, in the conduct and operation of the revolutionary tribunals, in the laws under which arrests were made and in the treatment of those arrested.

Under the law of 19 March 1793, the first Law of Suspects, which signalled the start of the Reign of Terror, those arrested were to be tried and executed within 24 hours with neither involvement of a jury nor the right to appeal. The Law of Suspects of 17 September 1793 no longer required actual evidence of carrying arms or of royalist support; reported expression or behaviour became enough. The law of 22 Prairial (10 June 1794) ended the, by then meaningless, right to defence counsel and witnesses – St Just's 'phantoms' (Greer, 1966: 20) – and made the death penalty the sole penalty of appearing before the Tribunal.

Other than official executions, it is estimated that at least 12,000 people were executed without even the pretence of a

> *Other than official executions, it is estimated that at least 12,000 people were executed without even the pretence of a trial: many were shot by those who had made the arrest*

trial: many were shot by those who had made the arrest – prosecutor, judge, jury, executioner all in one – and others were simply hanged from lampposts by mobs. A notorious incident was the drowning of around 2,000 victims when barges used as makeshift prisons were sunk in the cold waters of the river Loire. Adding to these victims, the conditions in prisons, with their makeshift nature, their overcrowding and their diseases such as dysentery, typhus and cholera, had the effect of condemning to death large numbers of those held within them, including those held before trial. The large warehouse at Nantes, for example, at one point held 10,000 prisoners.

Another compelling example of innocents being victims of terror is provided by the Soviet Union during the Great Terror, 1936–38. Under Stalin, people were frequently arrested without ever being charged with any offence. Following arrest, in ways similar to the conduct of the revolutionary tribunals in France, the arrested were often tried in groups, randomly brought together, with no protection from the law. Not only was 'suspicion' sufficient but, as stated by Article 22 of the 'Principles of Criminal Jurisdiction' in the Basic Criminal Code of the Soviet Union:

Punishment in the form of exile can be applied by a sentence of the State Prosecutor against persons recognized as being socially dangerous,

without any criminal proceedings being taken against these persons on charges of committing a specific crime or of a specific offence and, also, even in those cases where these persons are acquitted by a court of the accusation of committing a specific crime.
(Conquest, 1971: 425)

Hundreds of thousands of people passed before the Special Boards without rights to either defence or to appeal, and cases were brought not only against groups of people at a time without specific charges but also in absentia. Punishments were also severe, with 'corrective labour' mostly meaning death in a labour camp. Furthermore, those sentenced by the Special Boards were but a proportion of the millions who were sent to labour camps or executed.

Contrasting Italy

Fascist Italy was different: in Italy guilt and innocence did operate; at least, they did so before 1943, the year in which the German SS arrived in Northern Italy. Fascist Italy was a repressive regime, not a terror regime (Gregor, 1982). Although the Special Tribunal for the Defence of the State, instituted in Italy on 25 November 1926, held trials that were far from the ideal of justice, its function was to intimidate, not to terrorize. From 1926 until 1943, when the fascist regime collapsed, only 47 death sentences were passed, and of the 5,619 people prosecuted, 998 were found innocent. This contrasts strongly with the Soviet Union, where it has been estimated that in respect of the Gulag system there had been one million executions, two million camp deaths and eight million people in the camps by the end of 1938 (Conquest, 1990). Even on lower estimates (Nove, 1993) the figures remain staggering: the official figures on deaths in the labour camps, released from the archives since the fall of communism in 1991, is 900,000 for the period 1930–53, of whom 681,692 were executed at the peak of the purges, 1937–38.

Italy also contrasts with Germany: under the fascists, between 1926 and 1943, no Jews were executed. Treatment of Jews changed from September 1943, following the arrival of the SS (the Nazi 'Protection Squads') in Italy, from which time a total of 7,495 Jews were deported, 6,885 of them killed by the Germans (Gregor, 1982). In stark contrast, in Germany, from Hitler's rise to power in 1933 to the end of Nazi rule in 1945, a total of 5,978,000 Jews were killed (Landau, 1992). In Germany, Jews could not escape Nazi persecution by changing their behaviour.

Terrorist groups

This targeting of innocent victims, the use of summary justice inherent in its indiscriminate and arbitrary nature, is the essence of terrorism, crucial to both terror regimes and terrorist groups. The fear generated by the inability of escape once caught in the terror's net and the gruesome treatment of victims was much the same for the lonely traveller in fear of being plucked by the Thugs for the delights of the Goddess Kali as for that felt by those caught up in the web of surveillance committees, revolutionary tribunals and people's armies as they descended in France in 1793–94 to exercise summary justice. Those in the market place in Ancient Palestine or in the towns and cities of the Seljuk Empire in fear of the dagger carried by the Zealot or the Assassin, respectively, would have felt terror in much the same way as Jews in Germany in the grip of Nazism or citizens of the Soviet Union at the height of the Great Purges. It is the same terror, from which there is no escape, that is also the essence of the anarchists' 'propaganda by the deed'.

Explosions designed to kill innocents, in public areas or on public transport, and shootings aimed randomly into public gatherings can be carried out not only by members of terrorist groups but also by extremist individuals. In such acts terror is involved, but terrorist groups, just like terror regimes, require organization, the 'system of terror' meant by the word 'terrorism' when it first entered the English language in 1793–94. That is to say, in order to perpetrate the attack on innocents, terrorist groups require a means for manufacturing or obtaining weapons or explosives, for planning and coordinating their clandestine action and for training and disciplining members. Importantly, as for the distinction between terror regimes and repressive regimes brought out in the contrast drawn between Stalin's Soviet Union and fascist Italy, terrorist groups too need to be differentiated from groups that use violence only against enemies in a situation of 'internal war', for intimidation.

Real enemies versus innocents

The targeting of enemies is very different from the arbitrariness of the deliberate attack on innocents. Real 'enemies' are members of the government or of the state machinery – politicians, police, judges, members of the armed forces, even

> *The targeting of enemies is very different from the arbitrariness of the deliberate attack on innocents*

those such as editors of state-owned newspapers or leaders of state-run social, political or economic organizations. In some situations, such as in civil war, they may include opposition armed forces that are not those of the state or militias with only loose connections to the government. Innocent people, those targeted by terrorist groups, include the passengers who just happen to be on that flight on the day when the aeroplane is hijacked, or those workers or shoppers who by chance are in the building or street where the bomb is exploded. This category of innocents clearly encompasses those sitting in the Café Terminus when Emile Henry's bomb went off in France, in 1894, and the passengers on the hijacked aeroplanes and those at work in the twin towers of the World Trade Center, in the USA in 2001.

That those targeted by groups fit within the category of potential 'enemies' does not, however, automatically rule them out from classification as terrorist groups. It follows from the arguments made about terror regimes that the treatment received by those kidnapped or held hostage, whether 'enemies' or not, also counts. As for regime terrorism, evidence of summary justice is also crucial for identifying terrorist groups. The kidnapping of people, whether 'top people' or ordinary people, who are then let go unharmed does not constitute evidence of a terrorist group in action. Evidence of deliberate killing or death through the conditions of imprisonment, mutilation or torture is needed. One such striking example is the execution of the West German businessman Hanns-Martin Schleyer who was taken hostage by the Red Army Faction, in 1977, and viewed by them as an 'enemy' because he had held high rank in Hitler's SS. He was suspended by piano wire in mimicry of the treatment handed out by those who took part in the attempt to assassinate Hitler in 1944.

A group that attacks only property or stages acts purely as publicity stunts and does not harm people is not a terrorist group. It is wrong, therefore, to call groups like Earth First!, which directs

> *A group that attacks only property or stages acts purely as publicity stunts and does not harm people is not a terrorist group*

action only at property, a terrorist group. The kinds of action in which Earth First! engages include hammering spikes into trees so that they cannot be felled for lumber and sabotaging the nuclear power industry by cutting power lines and causing black-outs. Similarly, even if the publicity stunt chosen appears to emulate the tactics of terrorist groups, this does not make the group a terrorist group. A noted example is that of Croatian separatists who hijacked a Trans World Airlines flight in September 1976: the hijackers were not carrying weapons and the hostages were released unarmed. A more recent example occurred in Athens, in December 2004. A bus was hijacked by two Albanians, who threatened to blow it up unless a ransom, equivalent to one million dollars, was paid. The hostages were released unharmed and the bag containing the 'dynamite' turned out, instead, to be full of cigarettes and croissants.

Guerrilla groups: terrorist versus freedom fighter

If a group that attacks only property and directs attacks against real enemies, not indiscriminately against innocents, is not a terrorist group, it follows that it is also wrong to view guerrilla groups as synonymous with terrorist groups. Such is usually done on the much mistaken but oft quoted grounds that 'one person's terrorist is another person's freedom fighter'. Terrorism is neither the same as guerrilla warfare nor a specific type of it. In guerrilla warfare the aim is to establish liberated zones in which the alternative revolutionary government can be set up and practised and the guerrilla army can be built for the eventual overthrow of the regime through military action against the existing state's armed forces. Liberation armies similarly engage against the state army in order to overthrow the government, such as a colonial regime. Although 'one person's terrorist' is not necessarily 'another person's freedom fighter', however, both guerrilla movements and liberation armies can choose to adopt terrorism as a strategy. If they do so, they change their nature. The use of terror is a choice and, if chosen, the movement or army or the relevant section that has made the choice turns itself into a terrorist group.

That terrorism is a chosen strategy, a choice that can be made by guerrilla armies, is clearly illustrated by the case of Sendero Luminoso (Shining Path) in Peru, a case that will be covered in greater detail in Chapter 7. While starting out as a revolutionary rural guerrilla organization, adopting a policy of developing support in the countryside and living amongst the peasants, in 1980 they chose terrorism as a strategy and by the end of 1982 they were tossing dynamite indiscriminately into public places. Soon they engaged in maiming and torture as well as killing innocents. The senderistas concealed their identities by wearing masks and large hoods when carrying out the terrorist acts and the Sendero Luminoso organization was based on a network of cells, each cell containing no more than five members and the cell's leader the only member with connection to the next level (McClintock, 1984). Crucially, however, not all guerrilla armies choose the route of terrorism.

Guerrilla movements are armed and their aim is to overthrow the state. Because they are illegal, and because the size of the groups are small in comparison with the size of the state's armed forces, their operation is clandestine and based on surprise attacks. As they grow in size and establish their bases in liberated zones they develop guerrilla armies, which, if and when necessary, engage in guerrilla warfare against the state's armed forces in civil war. This was the pattern adopted by Mao Zedong in China in the revolutionary campaign that brought the Communists to power in 1949. It was also the pattern adopted by many revolutionary and liberation movements in Africa, Asia and Latin America. The guerrilla army that targets state personnel and active opposition, not ordinary passive members of the population, and avoids inhumane treatment of captives, is not a terrorist group. If the warfare is between opposed armed forces – real enemies – then terrorism is not involved. It is in the nature of war that innocent people will be killed, unintentionally, but it is only where killing, torture and maiming are aimed deliberately at innocents that terrorism is present. In any case, it is not in the later civil war stage, where battles are waged openly between guerrilla and state army, but in the early clandestine stage that confusion is made between 'terrorist' and 'freedom fighter'.

One very clear example of a guerrilla movement that was never a terrorist group and that, though it developed a guerrilla army, never adopted the Maoist strategy of guerrilla warfare is the 26 July Movement, which overthrew the repressive dictator Fulgenico Batista and brought Fidel Castro to power in the Cuban Revolution of 1959. The 26 July Movement fought Batista's National Guard – armed soldiers, real enemies – using guerrilla tactics. Never fighting the enemy in open combat, the essential tactics involved mobility and surprise attacks. Although the densely forested and mountainous terrain of the Sierra Maestra was crucial to their strategy to overthrow the Batista regime they also employed the tactic of kidnapping foreign reporters. These reporters, however, were neither killed nor tortured but set free, unharmed.

> *The 26 July Movement's aims in capturing and then releasing the reporters unharmed were both to publicize the movement's cause and for those released to report favourably on their treatment*

The 26 July Movement's aims in capturing and then releasing the reporters unharmed were both to publicize the movement's cause and for those released to report favourably on their treatment. Demonstrating their revolutionary message through their behaviour was crucial to the Cuban guerrillas in winning support, both at home and abroad, and most especially among the peasants of the Sierra Maestra, where the guerrillas established their base. In sharp contrast to the brutality of the National Guard, strict guidelines were followed on the treatment of peasants. For example, food was not to be stolen but to be paid for in some way, such as in exchange for medical treatment. In similar vein, captured regular soldiers were also to be released unharmed, minus their guns and ammunition. As Castro explained his policy of releasing soldiers on Radio Rebelde in 1958: 'We do not wish to deprive these Cubans of the company of their loving families. Nor for practical reasons, can we keep them, as our food, cigarettes, and other commodities are in short supply. We hope the people of Cuba will understand our position in this respect' (Fidel Castro quoted in Fairbairn, 1974: 271).

Distinguishing terrorism and sabotage

In *Guerrilla Warfare*, based on his experiences in the Cuban revolution, Che Guevara distinguishes between sabotage, which he advocates as a very important tactic, and terrorism, which he explicitly argues against. He does so for both moral reasons (it is wrong to kill innocent people and also leads to large loss of life)

> *In* Guerrilla Warfare, *based on his experiences in the Cuban revolution, Che Guevara distinguishes between sabotage, which he advocates as a very important tactic, and terrorism, which he explicitly argues against*

and practical reasons (it is ineffective, cannot be calculated towards objectives and leads to the deaths of people needed for the revolution). So, he argues:

It is necessary to distinguish clearly between sabotage, a revolutionary and highly effective method of warfare, and terrorism, a measure that is generally ineffective and indiscriminate in its results, since it often makes victims of innocent people and destroys a large number of lives that would be valuable to the revolution.
(Che Guevara, *Guerrilla Warfare*, 1969: 26)

Ernesto 'Che' Guevara, 1928–67

Born in Argentina on 14 June 1928, Che Guevara graduated as a medical doctor in March 1953. As a student he had travelled around Latin America and had become acutely aware of people's sufferings under tyranny. In mid-summer, 1955, he met Fidel Castro, who had been recently released from prison, having served part of his sentence for leading the storming of the Moncado Barracks in Cuba, on 26 July 1953. The date gave the name to the guerrilla movement. In November 1956, Guevara set sail from Mexico in the *Granma*, together with Castro and other members of the 26 July Movement, to continue the campaign to overthrow the repressive dictator Fulgenico Batista. Although only 19 guerrillas were left alive following the landing on Cuba in December, from their rural base in the Sierra Maestra a guerrilla army was developed, based on peasants, which succeeded in overthrowing Batista by the beginning of 1959. A new kind of revolution had occurred – one not organized by a revolutionary party – and a new theory of guerrilla warfare, based on practice, had been developed. Guevara wrote *Guerrilla Warfare* in 1960. In the new Cuba he held the posts of president of the National Bank, director of the National Planning Board and, later, Minister of Industries. He also headed many delegations for the Cuban government abroad. In 1965 he left office and departed for Africa, to the Congo, in an unsuccessful attempt to train guerrillas to fight against Tshombe. In 1966 Guevara went to Bolivia in order to carry on fighting for revolution in Latin America. He was killed there in October 1967.

In his criticism of terrorism as a method of revolution, Guevara adds that it undermines chances for organizing mass action. Regis Debray, however, who fought in Bolivia alongside Guevara until 1967, when taken captive and Guevara killed, allows that so long as what he terms 'city terrorism' is subordinate to the fundamental struggle – 'the struggle in the countryside' – then it has 'a strategic value' (Debray, 1968: 74). He explains: 'it immobilizes thousands of enemy soldiers in unrewarding tasks of protection: factories, bridges, electric generators, public buildings, highways, oil pipe-lines – these can keep busy as much as three-quarters of the army.' It is clear that it is not the killing of innocents that Debray has in mind but sabotage.

This confusion over the tactics of urban guerrillas, sabotage as terrorism, is compounded by the Brazilian revolutionary Carlos Marighela, whose *Handbook of Urban Guerrilla Warfare* had a strong influence on Latin American urban guerrilla movements. He dispensed with the idea of the primary importance of rural guerrilla operations, the 'foco' so absolutely critical to Guevara's and Debray's theorizing, and advocated urban guerrilla warfare as a critical revolutionary means. Rather than arguing for sabotage as a way of keeping soldiers occupied, Marighela's theorizing was much in line with those who advocated 'propaganda by the deed' in the nineteenth century. He argued that the dramatic act provokes the state to retaliate with heightened repression and generates the support of the masses in revolutionary action. The strategy advocated was not intended as a deliberate attack on 'the common people' (Marighela, 1971: 112) – innocents. The targets mentioned, however, included not only the military and politicians but also those unarmed, such as American residents and businessmen. He also lists terrorism as one of the 'methods of action' along with execution, kidnapping and sabotage. Furthermore, Marighela (1971: 89) specifically states 'By terrorism I mean bomb attacks', and he adds, 'terrorism may also include destroying lives, and setting fire to North American business establishments or certain plantations.'

Carlos Marighela, 1911–69

A long-term member of the Brazilian Communist Party (PCB), which had been banned since 1947, Marighela broke with the Party in 1967, having attended a conference of the Organization for Latin American Solidarity (OLAS) held in Havana, Cuba, in the summer of that year. In Brazil, a highly repressive military coup had overthrown President João Goulart's elected government in 1964. Legitimate opposition effectively destroyed and alternative forms of opposition either not forthcoming or proving ineffectual, in early 1968 Marighela, together with Mario Alves who had also broken from the PCB, set up the Revolutionary Communist Party of Brazil with the aim of beginning an armed struggle. It began with the Action for National Liberation (ALN), led by Marighela, which was then joined in the revolutionary campaign by other armed groups. The tactics employed by the urban guerrillas included bank robberies for funds and kidnapping foreign ambassadors in order to bargain for the release of rebels held in prison. The violence soon escalated. Marighela was tracked down and killed by police in November 1969. By 1971 the ALN had been defeated, no match for the strength and extreme violence of the ruling regime in Brazil. Marighela completed *The Handbook of Urban Guerrilla Warfare* in June 1969. The first collection of his writings was published in early 1970, in France, and given the title *Pour la Libération du Brésil*; two months after publication it was banned by the French government.

NLF versus FLN

At the time of the Vietnam War, the National Liberation Front (NLF), the guerrilla army led by Ho Chi Minh, was vehemently accused of terrorism. For example, under the Kennedy administration a White Paper was issued in which the actions and nature of the NLF were described in the following way:

No tactic, whether of brutal terror, armed action, or persuasion,
is ignored. If mining a road will stop all transport, who cares that
a school bus may be the first vehicle to pass.
(US Government White Paper, December 1961, quoted
in Schultz, 1978: 77)

Similar views about the NLF were adopted by presidents Johnson and Nixon and were also supported by academic studies. Once the war was over, however, it became possible to assess events more objectively, including analysis of 2,400 interviews, reports and captured documents. This evidence showed that, rather than being indiscriminate, targets were carefully chosen and consisted of assassinations and kidnappings of South Vietnamese Government (GVN) officials, which occurred mainly in the early years (Schultz, 1978). These GVN officials included both central and local administrative staff, soldiers and personnel in the intelligence and security organizations. In the late 1950s to early 1960s the NLF executed around 15 such officials each week. Once in control of each village, the tactics were relegated to secondary importance, the building of peasant support becoming the prime strategy. That the NLF used violence against enemies, not innocents, is a conclusion that contrasts with the evidence of the use of indiscriminate violence by the South Vietnamese Government.

The conduct of the NLF in Vietnam also stands in contrast with that of the Front de Libération Nationale (FLN) in the Algerian revolution, 1954–62.

The Algerian National Liberation Front (FLN)

The *Front de Libération Nationale* (FLN) was formed in Algeria in 1954 to fight for independence from France. The FLN adopted its organization and nationalist strategy from the underground Organisation Spéciale (OS), which had been set up to organize an armed uprising, in 1950. In November 1954, the FLN opened its campaign for liberation with attacks on the French security forces in the form of small-scale bombings, shootings and raids throughout Algeria.

In June 1956 the leadership of the FLN, the *Comité de Coordination et d'Exécution* (CCE), took the crucial decision to add terrorism to the list of tactics to be used. By September 1956 there were 5,000 'shock troops' (*groupes de choc*) organized in the FLN's underground force – the *Zone Autonome d'Alger* (ZAA). In September 1956, the ZAA opened a terrorist campaign: not targeting French security forces but bombing public places where European youths gathered for recreation. This episode began 'the Battle of Algiers', lasting from September 1956 until autumn 1957. The 'battle' was essentially fought between the ZAA and French paratroopers, and although the ZAA was soon defeated the result was that urban terrorism went out of control and terrorism became the weapon used on both sides.

In August 1958, the FLN adopted a new strategy: it began to attack targets in France. These targets included police stations, munitions factories and oil refineries. These attacks were brought to a halt by the FLN's recently formed provisional Algerian Government, GPRA. In 1959, FLN terrorism then moved to bombing department stores in Algeria and in 1960 and 1961 attacks took the form of bus explosions. This, however, led to the development of an opposition terrorist group, the *Organisation d'Armée Secrète* (OAS).

In March 1962 the French government and the GPRA signed a ceasefire and Algerians were granted the right to decide their own future.

The FLN chose terrorism as a means; in crowded urban areas bombs or grenades would be exploded: innocents targeted as victims. Massacres were carried out, as in the killing of every male person in Melouza in 1957. Although individual victims were mostly chosen for their connection with the French colonial government – policemen, tribal authorities, administrators and so on – the FLN also extended its actions to anyone viewed as having cooperated with the French, socially, politically or economically. Furthermore, the methods of killing and maiming individuals were savage: some had their throats cut, others had their noses sliced off. Importantly, these terrorist acts were carried out not by uniformed members of FLN brigades but by militant individuals through an underground organization. The unpredictability of falling victim, which no changes of behaviour might correct, was a deliberate strategy.

Mouloud Feraoun, an Algerian novelist and schoolteacher, recorded his feelings in his diary at the time:

Nobody is sure of anything, it is truly terror. . . . Terror which rules mysterious and unexplainable. . . .

Each of us is guilty just because he belongs to a category, such a race, such a people. You fear that they will make you pay with your life . . . you are afraid of being attacked uniquely because nobody has attacked you yet.

(Mouloud Feraoun, quoted in Crenshaw Hutchinson, 1978: 26)

Mysterious and inexplicable as terrorism may appear to the victim, from the perspective of the perpetrator it is quite another matter.

Terrorism

Terrorism is a chosen strategy implemented through a system of summary justice: its essence is the deliberate targeting of innocents as victims.

Recommended reading

For a collection of works on the concept of terrorism, see Rosemary H.T. O'Kane, *Terrorism, Volume I* (Cheltenham: Edward Elgar, 2005). James Gregor, 'Fascism's Philosophy of Violence and the Concept of Terrorism', in David C. Rapoport and Yonah Alexander, eds, *The Morality of Terrorism* (New York: Pergamon Press, 1982), is especially recommended. For a pioneering work on the uses of terror with case studies of primitive African communities see Eugene Victor Walter, *Terror and Resistance: A Study of Political Violence* (Oxford: Oxford University Press, 1969). For the contrasting case of Italy, see the compelling work by Jonathan Steinberg, *All or Nothing: The Axis and the Holocaust 1941–43* (London: Routledge, 1991).

For a general work on guerrilla warfare, see Geoffrey Fairbairn, *Revolutionary Guerrilla Warfare: The Countryside Version* (Harmondsworth: Penguin, 1974). Carlos Marighela, *For the Liberation of Brazil* (Harmondsworth: Penguin, 1971), is a collection of his works. On Cuba, the fullest work by far is Hugh Thomas, *Cuba or the Pursuit of Freedom* (London: Eyre and Spottiswoode, 1971). For expansion on the Algerian FLN, see Chapter 7.

CHAPTER 3

Revolutionary reigns of terror

IT WAS REVOLUTIONARY REIGNS OF terror that first roused my interest in terrorism. In the simulation of hell created by the Jacobin Terror in France, 1793–94, which led to the word 'terrorism' first entering the English language, the 35,000 to 40,000 estimated victims represented one person out of every 630 who died as a direct victim of the terror. The population of France was just over 25 million at the time.

The Reign of Terror in France: the classic case

The Reign of Terror began on 9 March 1793 with the setting up of the Committee of General Security to take charge of internal security. At the same time Representatives on Mission, consisting of 82 deputies of the Convention (the Constituent Assembly was reformed as the National Convention after the king was overthrown in August 1792), were sent to the departments. The next day, the Paris Revolutionary Tribunal was created and a law was then introduced to begin the organization in the French communes of surveillance committees (also known as revolutionary committees). The Law of Suspects, which aimed at controlling counter-revolution, was also first introduced in March 1793 (it was this law that was strengthened in September, when mere suspicion of counter-revolution became sufficient reason for arrest).

On 6 April 1793 the Committee of Public Safety was set up to take charge of both internal and external affairs. The overlapping responsibilities between the committees of Public Safety and of General Security were symptomatic of the extemporized nature of the Jacobin regime and it led, in part at least, to its arbitrary nature, under which such large numbers of innocent victims suffered and died. The Committee of Public Safety was the more famous of the two committees, not least because Robespierre became one of its members in July. The 'people's armies' also came into being in the early months, with enrolments beginning in May, before the decree to set them up was proclaimed in June and long before the law to enact them, which was passed in September 1793. Though set up under the Committee of Public Safety, in practice they generally took orders from the Committee of General Security and the local surveillance committees.

During the winter of 1793–94 revolutionary tribunals, similar to the Paris Revolutionary Tribunal, were established in five other areas, although, in practice, the majority of victims were sentenced by the military or civilian commissions (also known as revolutionary, popular or extraordinary commissions), set up by the Representatives on Mission. Revolutionary justice was also administered by existing departmental criminal courts and if too lenient the Representatives on Mission sent important cases to Paris, especially after April 1794.

The Terror reached its peak between December 1793 and January 1794, with nearly half of all the official executions occurring during those two months. The end of the reign of terror came in July 1794, marked by Robespierre along with 21 of his close allies

> *The Terror reached its peak between December 1793 and January 1794, with nearly half of all the official executions occurring during those two months*

being sent to the guillotine. In August, the dictatorial powers of the Committee of Public Safety were ended, its responsibilities split between 16 committees; the law of 22 Priarial was repealed and the Revolutionary Tribunal was reorganized and required to take evidence of intention to commit a criminal act into account.

The pattern set by the Reign of Terror in the French Revolution, with its extemporized government, extraordinary revolutionary organizations, wide laws on counter-revolution and summary justice dispensed by the machinery of revolutionary terror – the courts, the trial procedures, the police and secret police systems and the makeshift prisons – is also found in the Russian Revolution.

The reign of terror in the Russian Revolution

In the Russian case, the reign of terror began little over a month after the Bolsheviks took power in the October Revolution (7 November 1917 on the new calendar). On overthrowing the provisional government, which had been in power since the

February Revolution (March on the new calendar) that had overthrown Tsar Nicholas II, the Bolsheviks set up a temporary central government: the Council of People's Commissars, Sovnarkom, with Lenin as chairman. On 20 December 1917 (on the new calendar) the All-Russian Extraordinary Commission for Combating Counter-revolution and Sabotage, the Cheka, was set up under Sovnarkom. The Cheka or Vecheka, the acronym for its full Russian title, was a secret police system and it soon also took over ordinary policing.

Summary justice began when the Cheka issued instructions that counter-revolutionaries and saboteurs were 'to be shot on the spot . . . when caught red-handed in the act' (Cheka instruction, 22 February 1918, Bunyan and Fisher, 1965: 576). An armed combat detachment of the Cheka was quickly formed. In September 1918 the list of those to be arrested was extended in a way reminiscent of the Law of Suspects of September 1793 in France. In addition to spies, agitators, speculators, buyers and sellers of arms and those leaving to join in counter-revolution, the All-Russian Central Executive Committee (VTsIK) of the Congress of Soviets resolution included the inherently arbitrary 'and all who inspired them' (resolution recorded in Carr, 1966: 176). District, provincial and frontier chekas soon spread across Russia. In addition to prisons, forced labour camps were set up, run jointly by chekas and the Commissariat for Internal Affairs. The Cheka also ran concentration camps.

In ways similar to events in France, as well as arresting suspects and sending them before the Revolutionary Tribunal or carrying out on-the-spot shootings, the Cheka also carried out mass killings by shooting or by drowning victims in barges. The scale of executions together with deaths through neglect and ill-treatment of prisoners are also similar to those in France. The official figure for 1918–20, given by Latsis, the chairman of the Ukraine Cheka, is 12,733. The full total of victims, including those who died in mass executions without trials or as a consequence of prison conditions, whether before or after trial, is put at around 140,000 (Leggett, 1981). As a proportion of the population size, which was around 103 million in 1917, the figures for France and Russia are remarkably similar. Similarities are again found in more recent revolutions.

Not every revolution had a reign of terror. Nicaragua, for example, did not after the revolution of 1979. You can read more in my *Revolutionary Reigns of Terror*, where, in addition to France, Russia and

> *Not every revolution had a reign of terror. Nicaragua, for example, did not after the revolution of 1979*

Nicaragua, the cases of England (the Puritans), America, Mexico, China, Cuba, Ethiopia and Iran are also covered. Ethiopia and Iran deserve particular attention. Not only are they the most recent examples, but they also show the greatest similarities with France and Russia and highlight important lessons about the causes of revolutionary reigns of terror.

The reign of terror in the Ethiopian Revolution

The revolution in Ethiopia began in February 1974. Four months later the Co-ordinating Committee of the Ethiopian Armed Forces, Police and Territorial Army – the Derg – took power. Mengistu was chosen to be the chairman of its coordinating committee. At first the Derg acted in coordination with the official regime but things soon changed and, in September, Emperor Haile Selassie was publicly deposed and a new revolutionary government was installed: the Provisional Military Administrative Council (PMAC), effectively a new name for the Derg. At first the government operated much as a military regime but in the summer of 1976 things changed.

The reign of terror began on 5 July 1976 with legislation introducing death penalties or up to life imprisonment for widely defined 'anti-revolutionary activities'. In the same month, local surveillance organizations (security squads) were developed within the urban neighbourhood associations, the kebelles, which had begun to be set up a little over a year earlier, similar to peasant associations set up in the rural areas. Each kebelle had its own people's tribunal for the settling of local disputes. By October claims were made that the PMAC had killed 1,225 people, tortured hundreds in concentration camps and carried out mass executions.

Mengistu Haile-Miriam, c.1939–

Mengistu was born some time between 1939 and 1942. His ethnic origins are also disputed but it is clear that they are somewhat mixed: this gave him an advantage in his election, in June 1974, as chairman of the coordinating committee of the Derg. At the time of his election he was a major in the army but soon he became lieutenant-colonel and first vice-president of the PMAC and, in December 1976, following the reorganization, he became prime minister. On 3 February 1977, President Teferi Banti and eight other members of the PMAC were killed by their fellow members. Eight days later, the PMAC returned to the name of the Derg and Mengistu was elected president, commander-in-chief of the armed forces and chairman of the General Congress, Central

Committee and Standing Committee. From July 1977 he developed his own party, the Seded (Flame), and at the end of 1979 began the construction of a single-party state through the process of organizing a new political party, the Party of the Working People of Ethiopia (COPWE). In 1991 he was ousted by combined rebel forces, the Ethiopian People's Revolutionary Democratic Front (EPRDF), which won elections to the Constituent Assembly in 1994.

After Mengistu became president in 1977, some kebelles were armed and, in late April, a decree enabled people simply suspected of sabotage to be detained. Soldiers were empowered to dispense what they called 'revolutionary justice' (Markakis and Ayele, 1978: 167): summary justice. On 1 May (known as 'Bloody 1 May') events turned into a bloodbath. In just one concentration camp an estimated 600–1,000 students were massacred. The peak of the terror occurred from November 1977 through to the spring of 1978. It followed a government radio broadcast, on 11 November, which told 'all peasants, workers and progressive Ethiopians' to 'strengthen the struggle against counter-revolutionaries' and to 'spread Red Terror in the camp of reactionaries' (recorded in *Keesing's*, 1978: 28761). By early 1978, 300 of the armed kebelles had their own prisons, torturers and death squads.

Accurate figures of the terror are impossible to collect, but pieced together the evidence paints a gory picture. 'Counter-revolutionaries' were summarily executed by the police or death squads organized by the regime, with allegations of 3,500 people 'assassinated' in January 1978 and around 100–150 people being killed every night during February and March 1978. An Amnesty

> *An Amnesty International report published in November 1978 estimated that in the capital city, Addis Ababa, the Red Terror of December 1977 to February 1978 had produced around 5,000 deaths and that, in March 1978, 30,000 people were held in prison in very poor, crowded conditions with incidents of torture*

International report published in November 1978 estimated that in the capital city, Addis Ababa, the Red Terror of December 1977 to February 1978 had produced around 5,000 deaths and that, in March 1978, 30,000 people were held in prison in very poor, crowded conditions with incidents of torture.

The Terror had passed its peak by May 1978 and by the end of 1978 Ethiopia was under Mengistu's personal dictatorship.

The reign of terror in the Iranian Revolution

The Terror in the Iranian Revolution began shortly after Ayatollah Khomeini took power in February 1979, the Shah having left Iran in January in the face of the strikes, demonstrations and riots that had been raging since September 1978.

Ruhollah Mousavi Khomeini, 1902–89

Born in 1902 (1320 AH) in Khomein, son of the town's chief clergyman, Khomeini also entered the clergy. In 1941 he published *The Secrets Revealed* against secularization and the Shah's rule; before the decade was out his hostility to the Shah was public knowledge. He became a hojatalislam in 1945 and gained the higher rank of ayatollah in 1961. Following demonstrations against the Shah in 1962, Khomeini was arrested; once released his fame grew through radical speeches. Again arrested and imprisoned and, not long after his release, arrested once more, he was exiled to Turkey, later moving to Iraq, where he lived for 13 years. In 1971 he published *Al-Hukumah Al-Islamiya: Wilayat Al-Faqih (Islamic Government: Rule of the Religious Jurist)*. This was the work in which he outlined ideas for a Shia Islamic State. In 1978 he was expelled from Iraq and went to live in Paris, France. Once there he used the international media to his advantage and formed the Revolutionary Islamic Council in January 1979. He returned to Iran on 1 February; the revolutionary overthrow was achieved ten days later when the military command declared in his favour. Under the new constitution, put to a referendum in November 1979, Grand Ayatollah Khomeini gained supreme power as the Wali Faqih (Supreme Jurisprudent), which he remained until his death in 1989.

Alongside a new provisional government Khomeini set up the Revolutionary Islamic Council (IRC), centred in the holy city of Qom. The organizations of terror were controlled not by the provisional government but by the clerics through the Komitehs, the mosque leader committees, which had formed to fight the revolution and were now fully armed and greatly expanded in number. The Terror began immediately with summary trials held by extemporized Islamic revolutionary courts, followed by 600 executions. After a short suspension of proceedings, in April the revolutionary courts were reconstituted, each to be chaired by a religious judge. Further vague offences were added, including 'crimes against the revolution'. Summary trials and executions continued. By the end of March 1979 there were an estimated 20,000 political prisoners.

On 5 March 1979, a paramilitary police force that combined being an army and police force with being representatives of the mosque was formed – the Islamic Revolutionary Guard (IRG). Six months later a new secret police force, SAVAMA, was formed. During 1979 the Islamic Republican Party (IRP), which was first set up in February, became established and the Hezbollah, a thuggish force with veiled links to the IRP, made their first appearance.

The Terror escalated during 1981: from June 1981 the revolutionary guards and the hezbollahi made hundreds of arrests and carried out executions on the spot

The Terror escalated during 1981: from June 1981 the revolutionary guards and the hezbollahi made hundreds of arrests and carried out executions on the spot. Official executions also mounted and by the end of the year the number announced reached 2,500. In September 1981 the new Revolutionary Prosecutor-General had recommended that demonstrators should be executed on the same day that they were arrested whenever two witnesses could be found. In practice, executions were indiscriminate (Bakhash, 1985). There are no official figures published of the numbers executed in this way. The total officially recorded judicial executions since the revolution stood at 4,400 by July 1982. It was reported that no case was known of a defence lawyer being available, that prisoners were subject to torture and that prison conditions were appalling, with up to 80 prisoners per cell (*Keesing's*, 1982: 31798). Although the level of terror reduced by the end of 1982, the revolutionary reign of terror carried on until the beginning of 1984, when the revolutionary courts were brought under the Ministry of Justice.

Explaining reigns of terror

France

What provoked the setting up of the system of terror in the French Revolution was the outbreak of civil war in the Vendée, in March 1793. By April, it had spread throughout the West and soon erupted elsewhere. From May, anti-Jacobin rebellions (the Federalist Revolts) began, first in Lyon, where people faced starvation due to a crisis in the silk industry, and then in Marseilles and Bordeaux. The civil war remained critical to the terror: fully 76 per cent of all executions occurred in the departments where insurrections involving 1,000 or more people took place (Greer, 1966). Furthermore, the steep rise in victims at the peak of the terror between December 1793 and January 1794 was due to the punishment of rebels as the Jacobins won their decisive victories, beginning with the taking of Lyon through to the ending of the civil war in the West (aside from some outbursts in the Vendée, which continued into the spring).

Foreign war and economic crisis also played their parts. It was not the Jacobins who made the decision to go to war: it was made before they took power, when the Girondins, the moderates, dominated the Assembly and the king was in place as a constitutional monarch. The counter-revolution in the Vendée was triggered by the decision, on 24 February 1793, to conscript 300,000 men to fight in the war, but the underlying problem in the area was economic. Shortages of goods threatened starvation and had already provoked a short-lived uprising in September 1792. Unfulfilled government promises to resolve the problems had exacerbated grievances. The shortages and the threat of famine that they brought also lay behind the wider outbreaks of insurrection, which thrust the Jacobin regime deeply into crisis. Throughout 1793–94 large towns especially and Paris in particular were on the edge of famine.

The Jacobins sought to address the problems of supply and the threat of starvation in the towns by introducing legislation to control prices but their policies served to aggravate the civil war. In September 1793 they introduced the General Maximum to fix maximums on both prices and wages. The people's armies were used not only to fight counter-revolution and to protect public safety but also to protect supplies and ensure distribution of goods, food especially and grain in particular, to the urban markets. The people's armies frequently used excessive force when requisitioning and the effect was to turn the peasants against the urban population. The view of the people's armies as 'the terror on the move' was also aggravated by the dechristianization campaign, which, though started before the Jacobins came to power, stirred up widespread resistance when the requisitioning of materials from churches by the people's armies frequently turned to anarchical violence.

Not only did the use of excessive force to implement economic policies stir up counter-revolution in the countryside; it also aggravated resistance in the towns

Not only did the use of excessive force to implement economic policies stir up counter-revolution in the countryside; it also aggravated resistance in the towns. The uprising in Paris, which brought Robespierre and other Jacobins to the guillotine on the night of 9 Thermidor and so an end to the reign of terror, was provoked by the Paris Commune's publication, four days earlier, of a list of Maximum wage rates. They represented a substantial cut in workers' wages. This cut in wages, furthermore, occurred at a time of rising prices. From April 1794, the civil war by then essentially brought under control, the government had lost interest in violations of the Maximum in all foods other than bread. Robespierre had moved his focus to a spiritual approach and concentrated on the setting up of the Republic of Virtue. Its lack of popularity and the popular preference for practical solutions was demonstrated by his fall.

Russia

In Russia, the lessons of the French Revolution and of the terror that followed, and not least the lessons of Thermidor, informed Bolshevik thinking. In *Terrorism and Communism* (1961, first published in 1920) Leon Trotsky, leader of the Military Revolutionary Committee of the Petrograd Soviet, which over-threw the provisional government in the October Revolution of 1917, defends the Russian Communists against the accusation that terror followed naturally from the Marxist notion of 'the dictatorship of the proletariat'. Trotsky points out that the con-ditions faced by the Jacobins – foreign war and supporters of the old regime fighting within France – were similar to the problems faced by the Bolsheviks in Russia. In contrast to France, which was involved in foreign war until Napoleon Bonaparte's defeat in 1815, the end to the war promised by the Bolsheviks was negotiated with Germany under the Brest–Litovsk peace treaty signed in March 1918. The continuation of the First World War ensured that the Allies were too engaged elsewhere to support any serious invasion of Russia. Once the war was ended, in November 1918, the threat of invasion that loomed large in Bolsheviks' minds never materialized on any serious scale. Their major problem, as in France, was civil war.

The civil war began in the summer of 1918 with the eruption of peasant uprisings. It essentially consisted of three White army advances – from Siberia (defeated in July 1919), from the south (defeated in November 1919) and from the north-west (defeated in December 1919) – and an attack from Poland into the Ukraine (April to October 1920), which combined with renewed uprisings. From late summer 1920, peasant rebellions revived and spread combining with political oppositions such as Left Socialist Revolutionaries and Anarchists. The Tambov rebellion broke out in August 1920 and was not fully suppressed until April 1921; civil war also revived in the Don and Ukraine. Towards the end of 1920, worker rebellions, too, began to erupt in the Red areas, including within Moscow and Petrograd, with soldiers also becoming rebellious. In February 1921 there were a total of 118 separate uprisings, culminating in the famous rebellion in Krondstadt, the stronghold of the Boshevik Revolution.

As in France, the need to get food to the starving cities was crucial, but Bolshevik policies went far beyond anything attempted by the Jacobins. The policy, known as 'war communism', involved both the forcible collection of food supplies from peasants to feed the cities and the nationalization of all industries and banks. In a way similar to France and the role of the people's armies, the chekas guarded distribution networks and arrested those suspected of hoarding and profiteering. A revolutionary 'tax in kind' was also introduced, under which everything above a calculation of family need was requisitioned. The chekas procured grain through force. At first prices were fixed but this gave way to rationing. Wage-fixing was also introduced with a money economy eventually ceasing to exist. War communism collapsed in August 1920 and it was this economic crisis that accounts for the starving peasants reviving their rebellions from that point and also for the strikes and demonstrations becoming a serious and growing problem in the cities.

The civil war ended in March 1921 and, in contrast to Robespierre's metaphysical idea of the Republic of Virtue, Lenin introduced new practical economic policies: the New Economic Policy (NEP), which restored some important market mechanisms. The Bolsheviks remained in power to establish single-party Communist rule which, along with the NEP, was begun at the Tenth Party Conference held in March 1921. Three months later the Cheka's powers were cut and, in February 1922, it was replaced with the GPU (State Political Administration).

Ethiopia

In Ethiopia, the reign of terror followed the pattern of France and Russia: it, too, was primarily the consequence of civil war, aggravated by coercive revolutionary policies. In 1974, the Eritrean Liberation Front

> *In Ethiopia, the reign of terror followed the pattern of France and Russia: it, too, was primarily the consequence of civil war, aggravated by coercive revolutionary policies*

(ELF, a guerrilla secessionist movement first organized in 1961) and the Eritrean People's Liberation Forces (EPLF, which had broken from the ELF in 1970) joined forces to renew their rebellion. In addition to the liberation movements in Eritrea, 10,000–15,000 guerrillas of the Ethiopian Democratic Union (EDU, which was formed in March 1975 by liberal noblemen) took up arms against the Ethiopian Army in the bordering provinces of Tigray and Gonder. Protest from landowners was also widespread, with rebellion breaking out in the Wollo province, and by April 1976 Mengistu publicly acknowledged rebellion in all but three of the remaining provinces of Ethiopia. It was soon after this that the PMAC introduced the legislation that began the revolutionary reign of terror, in July 1976.

As in France and Russia, strikes and protests also erupted in the towns and cities. Two rival Marxist political factions were involved: the Ethiopian People's Revolutionary Party (EPRP) favoured a civilian party-led revolution, while Meison (All Ethiopia Socialist Movement) accepted the need initially for a military path to revolution, and therefore gained the backing of Mengistu's faction of the PMAC (some of whom were Meison members). The EPRP, having developed its own military branch, the Revolutionary People's Army, launched its destabilization campaign in September 1976. Several Meison leaders were killed. Meison in turn developed its own 'execution squads' and, finding itself surrounded by rebellions in nearly every province, turned the situation within Addis Ababa into civil war. The civil war then stirred up the threat of foreign war.

With the backing of the Somali government, the Western Somalia Liberation Front (WSLF) attacked Ethiopian troops in the Ogaden region in June 1977. By August, parts of southern

Ethiopia had also been taken over by Somali forces or by the WSLF. Somali troops withdrew from Ethiopia in March 1978 and, the WSLF defeated, civil war in the Ogaden ended. With opposition forces in Addis Ababa beaten into submission by May 1978, the Ethiopian army then turned its attention on Eritrea. By the end of 1978, the secessionist problem had been restrained and the Derg had achieved relative stability with Mengistu the undisputed leader.

The rivalry between the factions within the PMAC indicates that the policies chosen by the PMAC also had an impact on the eruption and spread of the civil war. The policies first initiated by the Provisional Military Administrative Council in December 1974 were a combination of state socialist and nationalist: 'Ethiopia First' the slogan of the revolution; the country to be one nation, with one culture, one religion, one language. All financial institutions and foreign companies were to be nationalized, industry to be under state control and ownership of land to belong to those working on it. The Marxist vision was that of Stalin's forced collectivization and nationalization, not Lenin's NEP. The land was brought under state ownership in March 1975, following which collectives and state farms were created and the peasant associations formed. These policies led to both resentment and shortages.

As a region traditionally incapable of growing sufficient to feed its population, Eritrea was especially hurt by the shortages; this was why

> *As a region traditionally incapable of growing sufficient to feed its population, Eritrea was especially hurt by the shortages; this was why protest had erupted there so quickly*

protest had erupted there so quickly. In August 1975 Ethiopian troops had embarked on a neutralization campaign in Eritrea. It was also in reaction to the land reforms that some of the great landowners formed counter-revolutionary forces. Peasants also began to hoard their produce; new famines then threatened in the provinces of Tigray and bordering Wollo; and so the problem of feeding the towns and cities became acute. The whole system of trade and transport collapsed, hitting production in the new large mechanized farms, and Addis Ababa was put at the brink of starvation. In July 1975 urban land and houses owned as investments were also nationalized, the kebelles, like the peasant associations, initially set up to administer rents and resolve local issues.

The problems in the regions were additionally aggravated by the literacy campaign, the zemacha, begun in October 1974 by students and teachers. These urban outsiders were resented, particularly where the nationalities felt threatened by the 'one nation' government. Under the state of emergency of 30 September 1975, military officers had been posted as governors in troublesome areas. The military had then embarked on operations against the landlords and their supporters, most notably in Wollo. So civil war had spread through most of the regions, had broken out in Addis Ababa and had, finally, stirred up foreign war.

Iran

In Iran, too, civil war, largely provoked by government policies, pushed the reign of terror to its peak with, again, foreign war contributing. In Iran, however, it was not economic policies creating acute economic shortages that were important but Khomeini's vision of a Shia Islamic Republic. During the early stage of the terror, the Islamic Revolutionary Council under Khomeini, as well as setting up the Islamic Revolutionary Guard, the new secret police SAVAMA and the Islamic Republican Party with its veiled links to the Hezbollah, took crucial steps towards the formation of the Islamic Republic. The new constitution was introduced on 14 November 1979: it set down that shi'ism was to dominate the state and the Wali Faqih (Supreme Jurisprudent) was to have supreme power.

As in Ethiopia with the reaction to the 'one nation' policy, fighting for regional autonomy began soon after the revolution. In March 1979 fighting broke out both in Kurdistan and in the Turkoman area; in April, Kurds and Azeri-speaking Turks clashed in West Azerbaijan and government troops sent to the area sided with the Turks, stirring deep resentment against the new regime. In August, fighting broke out between Kurdish guerrillas and the Islamic revolutionary guards. By then, regional Arab minorities had also staged demonstrations. These incidents were put down by force and led directly to the expansion of the Islamic Revolutionary Guard. In March 1980, fighting again broke out in Kurdistan and around 45,000 Iranian soldiers and almost as many revolutionary guards were sent against the Kurds. In September 1980, full-scale war broke out between Iran and Iraq.

Following the introduction of the new constitution, presidential elections were held in January 1980, but Dr Bani-Sadr, representing a liberal religious approach, won a resounding victory over the IRP candidate. As president, he became commander-in-chief of the armed forces. In the parliamentary elections to the Islamic Consultative Assembly (Majles) that followed in March 1980, however, the Islamic Republican Party gained the majority and Khomeini swung the balance by appointing the leader of the IRP as head of the Supreme Court. In June 1981, Khomeini ordered Bani-Sadr's dismissal as head of the army and the Majles voted to impeach him. Following his impeachment urban guerrilla warfare and street demonstrations broke out throughout the country. Lasting from June 1981 to September 1982, primarily Mojahedin but also Fadayan guerrillas pitted against revolutionary guards and hezbollahi. Bombings and assassinations escalated.

The Mojahedin, who had fought to overthrow the Shah, were generally sympathetic to the liberal theological thinker Shariati rather than Khomeini and supported Bani-Sadr. The Fadayan, who, like the Mojahedin also fought a guerrilla campaign against the Shah's regime, were Marxist-Leninist. After the revolution the majority of the Fadayan supported the Tudeh Party, the communist party of Iran, which had given its support to the Islamic Republic. The remainder, however, fought alongside the Mojahedin. In addition to the urban guerrilla warfare, in November 1981 fighting intensified in Kurdistan and in April 1982 the revolutionary guards launched a major attack. With the Mojahedin effectively broken by January 1983, Khomeini then turned his attention against the non-violent internal opposition, most notably the Tudeh Party. On 22 August 1982, fundamentalist Shia Islam was enshrined in law. Ayatollah Khomeini remained in power as the Supreme Jurisprudent over the Islamic Republic.

Conclusion

Revolutionary reigns of terror are extemporized governments; they are epitomized by summary justice. They construct a system of terror in order to impose centralized control with the aim of establishing a permanent post-revolutionary state. They occur at times of national and international crisis, civil war

Revolutionary reigns of terror are extemporized governments; they are epitomized by summary justice. They construct a system of terror in order to impose centralized control with the aim of establishing a permanent post-revolutionary state

being the major problem compounded by the revolutionary government's choice of policies and the coercion used to enforce them. The shocking scale of deaths and suffering reached by these revolutionary reigns of terror is evident but, shocking as these cases are, the levels of terrorism are surpassed by governments of a more established kind: those to which the term 'totalitarian regime' is applied.

Recommended reading

For expansion on these and other cases of revolutionary reigns of terror, see Rosemary, H.T. O'Kane, *The Revolutionary Reign of Terror: The Role of Violence in Political Change* (Aldershot: Edward Elgar, 1991). The classic work, which covers the French, Russian, American and Puritan revolutions, is Crane Brinton, *The Anatomy of Revolution* (New York: Vintage Books, 1965). I challenge his claim that America had a revolutionary reign of terror and offer a new general explanation. On the Reign of Terror in France, the major work is Donald Greer, *The Incidence of the Terror During the French Revolution: A Statistical Interpretation* (Gloucester, MA: Peter Smith, 1966). For an excellent short work, see D.G. Wright, *Revolution and Terror in France* (Harlow: Longman, 1974). For the Russian case the major work is George Leggett, *The Cheka: Lenin's Political Police* (Oxford: Clarendon Press, 1981). As for all aspects of the revolution E.H. Carr, *The Bolshevik Revolution 1917–23* (Harmondsworth: Penguin, 1966) is also recommended, especially vols. I and II.

On Ethiopia, René Lefort, *Ethiopia: An Heretical Revolution?* (London: Zed Press, 1983), and Christopher Clapham, *Transformation and Continuity in Revolutionary Ethiopia* (Cambridge: Cambridge University Press, 1988), are particularly valuable. There are many more books on Iran, but Ramy Nima, *The Wrath of Allah* (London: Pluto Press, 1983), Shaul Bakhash, *The Reign of the Ayatollahs: Iran and the Islamic Revolution* (London: I.B. Taurus, 1985) and Dilip Hiro, *Iran Under the Ayatollahs* (London: Routledge and Kegan Paul, 1985) are especially recommended.

CHAPTER 4

Totalitarian regimes

TOTALITARIAN REGIMES ARE CLOAKED in secrecy. Unlike revolutionary terrors, which are extemporized regimes arising out of post-revolutionary chaos, totalitarian regimes have the outward appearance of being established and legitimate. The unearthing of the true nature of the Nazi regime after the end of the Second World War, the spread of communism in Eastern Europe and growing understanding of the nature of the

Totalitarian regimes are cloaked in secrecy. Unlike revolutionary terrors, which are extemporized regimes arising out of post-revolutionary chaos, totalitarian regimes have the outward appearance of being established and legitimate

Soviet Union under Stalin led to theorizing about totalitarianism as a new type of government. This form was not simply new but intrinsically modern, a purely twentieth-century phenomenon, and common to both right wing and left wing extremes.

The most widely used concept for this new kind of government was that of 'totalitarian dictatorship' (Friedrich and Brzezinski, 1965). It was applied not only to the Soviet Union and Nazi Germany but also to Mussolini's Italy, all the countries of communist Eastern Europe, communist China, Castro's Cuba and even Ghana under Nkrumah. Totalitarian dictatorship is a syndrome of six characteristics: an ideology in pursuit of a completely new society and taking over the world; a single mass party led by a dictator through a state bureaucracy; a system of terror run by a secret police under party control; a monopoly of communications; an approximate monopoly of arms; and central control over the economy.

The end of communism in Eastern Europe and the Soviet Union and the opening of their archives revealed what many had argued all along: that there were important differences between these regimes, not least in terms of the treatment and toll of victims. The definition of terror used – 'a process in which activities of deliberate violence are undertaken by the power wielders to strike general and undefined fear into anyone who dissents' as 'a deliberate policy to intimidate' (Friedrich and Brzezinski, 1965: 170) – had drawn in cases that though repressive were not terror regimes.

In *The Origins of Totalitarianism*, Hannah Arendt took a far more restrictive view of totalitarianism; for her only Stalin's Soviet Union and Nazi Germany, and then only from 1930 and 1938 respectively, qualify as 'fully-fledged totalitarian regimes'. While she views Mussolini's Italy as a totalitarian dictatorship, though even here only from 1938 onwards, she is adamant that Mussolini 'did not attempt to establish a fully-fledged totalitarian regime and contented himself with dictatorship and one-party rule' (Arendt, 1958: 308). A totalitarian regime, though a modern, twentieth-century phenomenon, is unlike totalitarian dictatorship in that it is run from behind the state, not through it, and terror is directed not at dissidents but at innocents.

In Arendt's conception of a totalitarian regime, 'real power' (as opposed to the 'ostensible power' of state institutions) belongs to the secret police – 'the power nucleus' (p. 420) – with concentration camps at the core of their operation, the whole system characterized by lawlessness. The state is a façade, a shapeless creation of 'multiplication of offices' and 'duplications

---

Hannah Arendt, 1906–75

Hannah Arendt was one of the major political thinkers of the twentieth century. A German by birth, an intellectual by nature and education, and with a doctoral thesis on Saint Augustine, she was initially uninterested in politics. Her rude awakening came from the realization that in Germany in the 1930s regardless of the unimportance of Judaism in her daily life and her intellectual interest in Christian theology she was, in the eyes of others, simply a Jew. In 1933, faced by many German intellectuals supporting Hitler she became involved in the Zionist movement. After a short time in police custody she left Germany to become a refugee in France; in 1941, after internment in a French camp, she escaped to the United States, where she lived for the rest of her life. She supported the campaign for a Jewish army to fight alongside the Allies but was strongly opposed to a Jewish state in Palestine if imposed on Arabs living there. *The Origins of Totalitarianism* was first published in 1951, with a more complete edition in 1958. Other major works include *The Human Condition* (1958) and *On Revolution* (1963).

of function' (p. 399) and even 'fake departments' (p. 371), a far cry from the centrally organized party-bureaucracy of the syndrome of totalitarian dictatorship. Behind the façade the system of terror operates in concealment. The primary purpose of terror in Arendt's totalitarian regime is not that it is aimed at dissidents in order to create fear but that it is directed deliberately at innocents in order to destroy spontaneity and achieve perfect obedience for the purpose of 'total domination'. She argues as follows:

Terror as we know it today strikes without any preliminary provocation, its victims are innocent even from the point of view of the persecutor. This was the case in Nazi Germany when full terror was directed against Jews, i.e. against people with certain common characteristics which were independent of their specific behaviour.

> *Terror as we know it today strikes without any preliminary provocation, its victims are innocent even from the point of view of the persecutor*

(Arendt, 1958: 6)

Jews did not 'dissent' by being Jewish; it was not an attribute that they could alter through a change of behaviour any more than was the case for Gypsies, homosexuals, mentally ill people or physically disabled people. Similarly, in the Soviet Union when dekulakization was taking place the classification as a kulak was based not on a precise, legalistic definition but only on the vague basis of social status before and after the revolution, which no change of behaviour could alter. The years 1930 and 1938 are chosen by Arendt as the crucial points of transformation into 'terror as a form of government' (p. 368) in the Soviet Union and Germany respectively because these years mark the dates when the concentration camps (and gulags) started to be overwhelmed with 'completely "innocent" inmates' (p. 450).

In addition to Stalin's Soviet Union, from 1930 to 1953, and Hitler's Germany, from 1938 to 1945, there is one other paradigm terror regime. The case is singled out in the recent German debate, the *Historikerstreit*: 'Democratic Kampuchea', more commonly known as Cambodia under Pol Pot.

The system of terror in Stalin's Soviet Union

In the middle of 1929, Stalin began to force peasants into collective farms and spoke of his desire to 'liquidate the Kulaks as a class' (Stalin quoted in Deutscher, 1968: 324). (Kulaks were wealthy

> *In the middle of 1929, Stalin began to force peasants into collective farms and spoke of his desire to 'liquidate the Kulaks as a class'*

farmers, also referred to as the rich peasants.) In January 1930, he issued a decree on dekulakisation; it involved expropriation of property, and expulsion from the village. In the same month a law was introduced on 'exile combined with corrective labour', the first of its kind. On 7 April 1930 a decree was issued that made it compulsory that anyone sentenced to more than three years and anyone sentenced by the GPU (State Political Administration) for whatever term had to be sent to a 'corrective labour camp'. In 1930 the GPU established a new department, the Chief Administration of Forced-Labour Camps – the GULAG.

On Soviet estimates, as many as 600,000 farms were dekulak-ized in the years 1930 and 1931, and as many as 1.8 million people were exiled to remote regions of the USSR. By 1933 the number of farms collectivized probably reached 1.1 million or even higher. At first, those refusing to hand over their farms to collectives were arrested and their families were deported in cattle trucks under GPU guards to the White Sea area, where they were billeted with peasants. Under the sheer pressure of numbers new waves of deportees were housed in barns and then some even lived in holes in the ground before constructing their own mud huts. The term 'kulak' soon came to be used for any peasant who tried to resist the collection agents and then, from 1932, for anyone unable to contribute fully to the collec-tive (Viola, 1993). In August of that year, a law was introduced signed personally by Stalin, its full title 'On the defence of the property of state enterprises, collective farms and cooperatives, and the strengthening of social ownership'. Conviction under this law brought the death penalty, or ten years' imprisonment, which meant forced labour. The accusation of 'theft', even of small items, could result in extremely harsh punishments.

The initial makeshift arrangements gave way to a scheme for exiles to Siberia to develop nearly a million acres of land into collectives – 'special settlements' – to provide food for the towns and cities. In practice, they were forced-labour camps (Andics, 1969). The figures on deaths resulting from the journey and labour exploitation during the collectivization period can only be calculated roughly. A balanced assessment of all the estim-ates suggests that between 1929 and 1935 around 1,400,000 people died as a consequence of deportations and 3,306,000 died in the camps or in transit to them (Rummel, 1990). During these years the forced-labour camp system was expanded and established as a durable organization.

With collectivization effectively completed, in July 1934 the GPU was replaced by the new People's Commissariat for Internal Affairs, the NKVD. It retained the administration of the 'corrective labour camps' under the Gulag and the use of forced labour stayed central to the whole system. Within a few months all 'places of detention' and the exiles' camps were brought under the Gulag's control. The NKVD Special Board (or Special Tribunal) was also set up and was fully operational by the end of the year. Most of the accused were sentenced by a committee of the Special Board; it was rare for appearance to be before a court of law. Indeed, the Special Board explicitly laid down that it was to be given those 'cases for which the evidence was not sufficient for turning the defendant over to a court'.

The accused had neither right to defence nor right to appeal and were either tried in absentia or in groups at a time. Initially sentences were limited to five years but soon terms of eight or ten years were being imposed. Just being a relation or acquaintance of the accused could be enough. A case, quite typical, was that of the arrest of two engineers and their families because one of them had been sent a parcel from a relative in Poland: it contained nothing other than crayons, dolls and shoes. Even the engineer who had not received the parcel was sentenced to ten years (Conquest, 1971). In the lists of people drawn up for death by shooting, List No. 4 said simply 'Wives of Enemies of the People'. Arbitrariness also featured at the end of a Board sentence: the prisoner could simply be re-arrested.

In the summer of 1936 mass arrests took place of Left Oppositionists along with past and present associates. Show trials of Old Bolsheviks followed but the purges changed and escalated after Ezhov's appointment as head of the NKVD in September 1936. So began the Great Purges of 1936–38. Under Ezhov's direction, the terror expanded to include industrial managers, engineers and administrators at both the provincial and district level and the main accusation changed from conspiracy to kill Soviet leaders to economic sabotage, 'wrecking'. A new kind of camp appeared especially for workers who broke labour regulations: 35 such camps existed by the end of 1937 (Dallin and Nicolaevsky, 1948).

Though never formally announced, 'Troikas' were put into operation at the end of July 1937, with Ezhov and Vyshinsky, the Prosecutor-General, at their centre. The Troikas were established all over the Soviet Union, with the local NKVD chief as chairman. As with the Special Board, they operated terror under a veneer of legality. Defendants were not necessarily present at the proceedings: 40 per cent of all cases were held in absentia, and of those present their appearance averaged only three minutes. The Troikas could impose the death penalty and did so on a grand scale.

> *40 per cent of all cases were held in absentia, and of those present their appearance averaged only three minutes. The Troikas could impose the death penalty and did so on a grand scale*

In spite of the release of statistics on the terror from the Soviet archives, controversy remains over the figures. For example, Conquest (1990) has reaffirmed his original 'approximations' for 1937–38 as seven million arrests, one million executions (mostly shot) and two million camp deaths, giving about eight million in the camps at the end of 1938. On the other hand, Nove (1993) gives far lower estimates, recording the number of shootings following the trials and special tribunals as 353,074 in 1937 and 328,618 in 1938. The total for inmates in 1939 he puts at 3,593,000 in NKVD prisons, camps and colonies, with 1,360,000 of these in Gulag camps. Though the figures may differ, there is no dispute that the number of deaths reached its peak in the years 1937 and 1938. The number of people detained within the Gulag camps was at its peak, however, not during the Great Purges but in the early 1950s.

In 1938, Ezhov was purged along with other members of the NKVD. From then the number of executions fell sharply. Regulations on worker absenteeism, lateness and so on, however, soon became more punitive, and in June 1940 a decree introduced the seven-day working week along with harsh new laws on worker absenteeism and indiscipline. In 1945, at the end of the war, large numbers of new forced labourers were sentenced to the labour camps, which continued to expand in both size and number. By the end of Stalin's rule there were 131 camp groupings and a further 475 colonies and 667 labour camps besides. Between the beginning of 1934 and the end of 1952 over 18 million people entered the camps and colonies (Bacon, 1994), overwhelmed by innocent victims.

The system of terror in Hitler's Germany

In March 1933 the National Socialist German Workers' Party (NSDAP) took power in Germany and, in July, made itself the only legal political party. After 1933 the number of times the Reich Cabinet, the executive of the outward state, met declined sharply; it met for the very last time in February 1938.

During the years 1933–38, the SS organization, headed by Himmler, was developed as a terror system, outside of state control. The SS were the 'Protection Squads' of the NSDAP. By the end of 1933 Himmler had achieved control over every German state police force except the Prussian police, which remained a separate agency, as the political police – the Gestapo – organized under Goering. In April 1934, Goering appointed Himmler Inspector of the Gestapo and, although Goering remained its Chief, in practice Himmler was entirely in control of the secret police. The difference between Goering and the Gestapo and Himmler and the SS was that the Gestapo remained part of the state organization.

On 30 June 1934, Himmler was given total responsibility for all concentration camps. The small prisons and camps first set up in 1933 using buildings such as disused warehouses and factories to deal with all the political prisoners were replaced by large concentration camps. Sachsenhausen, near Berlin, was established in 1936 and Buchenwald, at Weimar, was established in 1937. Sachsenhausen and Buchenwald were modelled on Dachau, the concentration camp set up near Munich in March 1933. Whilst Dachau held mainly political prisoners, Sachsenhausen and Buchenwald became increasingly filled with 'asocials'. No comprehensive law on asocials was ever promulgated and classification as 'asocial' was, therefore, arbitrary. The SS had already perfected the practice of taking people off to concentration camps immediately after acquittal at trial or after completion of their sentence.

In the Basic Decree of December 1937 the function of the SS concentration camps had clear specification as 'state correction and labour camps'. Before his elevation to Inspector of the Concentration Camps and Führer

In the Basic Decree of December 1937 the function of the SS concentration camps had clear specification as 'state correction and labour camps'

of the SS Guard Units – the SS Death's Head Units – Eicke had been camp commandant at Dachau. The SS Death's Head Units guarded and ran the concentration camps. The Hitler Bodyguard Regiment, recruited from the SS and formed in 1933 (and strengthened in 1938–39), was also under Himmler's control. In June 1936 Hitler gave Himmler the new official title of Reichsführer SS and Chief of the German Police in the Reich Ministry of the Interior. From this point the criminal police began to be taken over completely by the SS and the power of the Minister of the Interior, Frick, passed, in practice, to Himmler.

In 1938, the Nazi regime completed its construction for a terror regime, Arendt's totalitarian regime. Early in the year the army command was changed and those regarded as political moderates who upheld the rule of law were also removed from ministerial positions. The changes in the army command removed resistance to the increase in the armed SS and enabled development of an entirely separate SS domain. On 9–10 November 1938, *Krystallnacht* ('Crystal Night', the night of shattered glass), Jews were beaten and murdered, synagogues were burnt, Jews' shops and homes were destroyed and

25,000 Jews were arrested and sent to concentration camps at Sachsenhausen, Buchenwald and Dachau.

In 1938 the Flossenbürg concentration camp was established followed by the camp at Mauthausen in 1939. Both had SS-owned enterprises attached run by forced labour. In the winter of 1941–42 the concentration camps were developed as an 'SS-owned arsenal of compulsory labour' (Broszat, 1968: 483). This occurred at the same time as the policy of extermination of 'undesirables' (a category that was especially applied to Jews) was put into operation. In 1941–42, extermination camps were set up in Poland, including Auschwitz II (Birkenau). From the summer of 1941, German and European Jews under German occupation were deported to the east and exterminated in the camps.

By August 1943 the total of concentration camp prisoners stood at 224,000, nearly treble the number at the end of 1942. A little over a third of these were in the three Auschwitz camp units – Auschwitz (I), Birkenau (II) and Morowitz (III). Birkenau was the main extermination camp; Auschwitz I was the main administrative camp, with labour there used to produce armaments; Morowitz was the labour camp that produced synthetic rubber and petrol. By April 1944, there were 20 concentration camps and 165 attached labour camps.

> *By the end of Nazi rule, in May 1945, when Germany signed the unconditional surrender in the Second World War, a total of 5,978,000 Jews had been killed*

By the end of Nazi rule, in May 1945, when Germany signed the unconditional surrender in the Second World War, a total of 5,978,000 Jews had been killed (Landau, 1992). Large numbers of other innocents – Gypsies, mentally ill people, incurably sick patients, homosexuals, Jehovah's Witnesses and 'asocials' – had also been killed. In addition, Poles and Russian workers (Slavs) and other foreign workers had been worked to death or died in transit to Germany (Homze, 1967).

The system of terror in Cambodia under the Khmer Rouge

Cambodia from April 1975 to January 1979 was, in much the same way as Stalin's Soviet Union and Nazi Germany, that rare form of regime in which a system of terror operates from behind the state, not through it, and in which terror is directed deliberately against vast numbers of innocents. Out of a population of a maximum 7.7 million, early estimates of the number of people killed as a direct result of Khmer Rouge policies during those years were put at around 1 million. Later estimates have put the death toll as low as just under 400,000 (Vickery, 1985) but also as high as 1,671,000 (Kiernan, 1996). In proportion to their populations even this lowest estimate is in line with those for Stalin's Soviet Union and Nazi Germany.

In April 1975, the National United Front of Cambodia (NUFC), which consisted of the combined forces of the Khmer Rouge and those loyal to Prince Sihanouk (who had been overthrown by General Lon Nol in the 1970 coup), succeeded in taking power. Immediately, the Khmer Rouge worked to consolidate their control and over the following months the Pol Pot faction strengthened its position, finally officially displacing Sihanouk's puppet government. A new constitution came into force in January 1976, naming the country 'Democratic Kampuchea' and creating a 250-seat 'National Assembly'. In April 1976, after elections in March under the new constitution, Pol Pot became prime minister and Khieu Samphan became president of the State Praesidium.

After the March 1976 elections the Assembly quickly 'dropped into obscurity' (Carney, 1989: 90). Apart from the

---

Pol Pot, 1925–98

Real name Saloth Sar, Pol Pot was born in 1925 (some sources record it as 1928) to a peasant family in Kompong Thom province, later moving to the capital, Phnom Penh. In 1949, after winning a scholarship, he went to Paris to study radio electronics but returned to Cambodia in 1953 after failing his exams. Earning income as a schoolteacher, he worked, unpaid, for the Kampuchean People's Revolutionary Party (KPRP). In 1960 he and his Paris student group took control of the KPRP, renaming it the Workers' Party of Kampuchea (WPK). In 1966 the WPK again changed its name, this time to the Kampuchean Communist Party (KCP), more commonly known as the Khmer Rouge.

The central body, headed by Pol Pot, was referred to as 'Ankhar' – 'Higher Organization'. After entering Phnom Penh in April 1975, Ankhar was given as justification for ordering people to evacuate the city and later for ordering people to their death. It was not until September 1977 that Pol Pot announced that the Communist Party had controlled the country since April 1975.

The Khmer Rouge was overthrown in January 1979 by a combined resistance movement and Vietnamese troops but Pol Pot was not captured and the Khmer Rouge maintained bases on the Thai border. He was captured by former supporters in 1987 and a 'people's tribunal' sentenced him to life under house arrest. He died in April 1998.

January 1976 Constitution, the Khmer Rouge issued neither laws nor decrees. In the newly named Democratic Kampuchea, government was carried out from behind the state and in the autumn of 1976 Pol Pot himself dropped out of the public eye to operate under complete concealment. On 27 September it was announced that Pol Pot had resigned for 'health reasons' and Nuon Chea, chairman of the standing Committee of the People's representative Assembly, became 'acting premier'. In practice Pol Pot was back as prime minister within the month, though not officially so until September 1977, when he made his declaration that the Communist Party of Cambodia had controlled the country since April 1975.

During those shadowy months, with the support of the south-western and northern military commanders, Pol Pot began an onslaught against other zonal armies; purges started in early 1977. At the crux of the regime was Tuol Sleng, the main centre for interrogation, torture and execution in Phnom Penh, and nucleus of Norkabal, the secret police system. Other 'prison-torture-execution centres' were to be found at regional, district and commune levels. The records at Tuol Sleng showed that of the 14,499 people held there between April 1975 and the end of 1978, only four survived. Elsewhere, victims met their death in mass executions carried out away from the population (Quinn, 1989).

Towards explanation

These cases share three things in common. Before the per-petrators of the terror took power each country had experienced dislocated societies, characterized by dramatic social and geographical movement, in part the consequence of high levels of death. Forced labour was a central plank of the terror regimes' economic policy, which was intertwined with the terror system. The economic crisis that the regimes faced when first in power was followed by a period of economic improvement and then renewed economic crisis.

> *Forced labour was a central plank of the terror regimes' economic policy, which was intertwined with the terror system*

Dislocated societies in Russia and Germany

By the early 1920s Russia had undergone enormous demographic changes and experienced dramatic social change. Beginning in the 1890s, rapid movement from rural to urban areas took place as a consequence of a government programme of fast industrialization. From 1914 Russia was embroiled first in foreign war (1914–18), then revolution (1917), then civil war (1918–21), then famine (1921). In the First World War approximately 1.7 million Russian soldiers were killed. In the period of revolution and civil war, 1917–21, an estimated ten million people lost their lives. During this time the number of people living in the cities then fell sharply: the population of Moscow fell by half, and that of Petrograd by two-thirds. The severe drought in 1921 brought famine to the Volga basin, the southern Urals and areas of the Ukraine. By the end of 1921, five million people had died of starvation. By 1920 the war communist economy collapsed, with inflation so high that the money economy had effectively ceased to exist.

A dislocated society also existed in Germany where, too, rapid industrialization occurred in the 1870s and 1880s. As in Russia, with the consequent growth in factories, rural workers migrated to towns and cities. As the rural workers moved out, so landowners replaced the migrating workers with foreign labour, particularly in Eastern Germany. By 1914, half a million foreign agricultural workers were seasonally employed there.

The war resulted in an estimated loss of 1.8 million German soldiers, the highest figure of any of the countries involved. Defeat in November 1918 brought a continuation and escalation of the social disorder that had begun in 1916 and it also led to economic chaos. Beginning with a mutiny at Kiel on 2 November 1918, spontaneous revolts began to break out elsewhere, the revolutionary impulse reaching Berlin by 9 November. Following the abdication of the Kaiser, a revolution through reform was begun by the Social Democratic Party, but between late 1918 and March 1920, with two subsequent outbursts in March 1921 and 1923, Germany experienced a further series of revolts and strikes led by those intent on full proletarian revolution. The economic crisis caused by the runaway inflation that followed the defeat in the war was added to by the reparation payments demanded by the Allies, some 33,000 million dollars. By June 1922, the value of the mark had dropped to just 1 per cent of its value in 1914, much as had occurred for Russian money between 1917 and 1921.

In both Russia and Germany, post-war economic crisis gave way to economic improvement but renewed economic crisis followed.

Renewed economic crisis

In the Soviet Union, economic reconstruction to repair the economic devastation brought by war, revolution and civil war in Russia began under the New Economic Policy (NEP) and was completed between the years 1925 and 1927. Contrary to plans, however, by the end of 1927, a severe shortage of goods developed. Unemployment was also rising sharply and, with urban unemployment approaching two million, tensions developed between the established workers and those pouring into the cities looking for work.

By the end of 1928 the level of grain procured under the 'extraordinary measures' introduced that year stood at less than two-thirds of the target. Economic crisis hit the USSR in 1929. Having expanded his power through the years, Stalin had by then moved to a position where he could impose his choice. His choice, for alternatives were available and ably supported (by Bukharin, for example), was for forced collectivization. By the end of the agricultural year, June 1929, the situation had grown worse and the grain procured had fallen by two million tons on the previous agricultural year. Panic developed in the cities and rationing was introduced as the country reverted to the crisis situation faced in the civil war. From the middle of 1929, Stalin moved fully to forced collectivization and also determined on heavy industrialization. So it was that in January 1930 the decree on dekulakization was formally set down and the new law introduced combining 'exile with corrective labour'.

January 1930 marked the start of terror as government in the Soviet Union. The forced-labour camps were developed, expanded and established, and the secret police system perfected. Economic crises, however, continued. A great famine occurred in 1933; shortages of labour in industry were endemic and, following an upturn in the economy in 1934–36, economic growth suddenly came to a halt, exposing shortages and short-falls in the economy. It was at

January 1930 marked the start of terror as government in the Soviet Union. The forced-labour camps were developed, expanded and established, and the secret police system perfected

this point that the Great Purges began.

In Germany, also, considerable economic recovery was achieved during the 1920s. Through a negotiated package of American loans and reduced reparation payments the economy stabilized. The economic background to Hitler's rise to power in 1933 was, essentially, set by the Great Crash of October 1929. In March 1930, the socialist chancellor resigned and Brüning (Centre Party) was given the task of forming a new government. Shunning the path taken by the socialists at the start of the Weimar Republic, Brüning chose to embark on deflationary poli-cies. Economic and political crisis ensued.

In April 1931 the Austrian credit bank owned by Rothschild collapsed; within a matter of weeks the Reichsbank had lost three billion RM and other German banks collapsed and foreign trade ceased. By the winter of 1930–31 unemployment reached five million, and by the following winter it reached six million, putting a tremendous strain on the system of unemployment pay. Votes for the Nazi Party rose dramatically in elections. In May 1932 Brüning resigned. After the elections that followed coalitions that excluded the Nazi Party could not be formed and on 30 January 1933, Hitler became chancellor with a nationalist coalition cabinet in which Nazis were a minority. Still without a majority of votes, this minority was turned into a majority in the March elections with support from the German Nationalist Party. On 12 November 1933 Hitler declared the Nazi Party the only legal party. So began the building of their system of terror, which was fully operational from 1938.

During 1933–38, Hitler appeared to achieve economic recovery for Germany, though published figures are 'misleadingly high' (James, 1987: 424). By 1938 economic problems were apparent: serious shortages of goods and labour, both skilled and agricultural, were revealed; real incomes were in decline; foreign exchange was in short supply; and deterioration in the quality of goods was also demonstrably cause for concern. Crystal Night occurred in November of that year.

Innocents as victims

Innocents were used both as scapegoats to deflect blame from the effect that both Stalin's and Hitler's policies had in renewing economic crisis and to provide sources of forced labour. In the Soviet Union, kulaks, widely defined, were blamed for the grain shortages; accusations of class enemies were especially acute in the famine-stricken areas of the North Caucasus and the Ukraine; newcomers to towns were potential scapegoats, later to be 'wreckers'. In the Great Purges, scapegoats were also made of those who had been Party members during the revolution and civil war. From 1940, the nationalities came to form an increasingly large proportion of the labour camp inmates and, after the war, soldiers returning home were sent on to labour camps.

In Germany, the legislation for the 'Restoration of the Civil Service', introduced in April 1933, both anti-Semitic and anti-communist in design, showed clearly who the Nazis chose to blame for economic crisis. Jews in Germany were a group traditionally blamed for economic problems. Further legislation discouraged Aryans from employing Jews. In 1935 the Nuremburg Laws were introduced in which Jews were excluded from citizenship. Along with the anti-Semitic laws other legislation and decrees were directed at 'alien races' and 'racially less valuable' members of the population such as the mentally ill. In Nazi racial-thinking Jews were at the bottom of the pile but Slavs and Gypsies were also *Untermenschen*, as too were those with mental or physical illnesses, which included, in Nazi thinking, all homosexuals and recidivists. The last such legislation, however, stopped in January 1937 from which point 'the regime preferred to solve the "question" without resorting to formal legislation or decrees' (Burleigh and Wippermann, 1991: 49). The 'final solution' to the 'Jewish question' was carried out in secrecy, behind the state, through the SS organization's system of terror, with concentration and labour camps at its centre.

Dislocated society in Cambodia

Although contrasting in many ways with Germany and Russia, and not least in respect of its level of development, Cambodia, too, had a severely dislocated society. Before the fall of Phnom Penh in April 1975, Cambodia was torn apart by both civil and foreign war. Millions of people left the countryside in order to escape the indiscriminate bombing and to avoid the starvation that threatened as a consequence of the destruction of agriculture in the war regions. Civil war began to build from the late 1950s. After an initial appearance in 1946 in the fight for independence from the French, guerrillas re-emerged in 1958, challenging Prince Sihanouk's government at various times to the mid-1960s. Following a peasant revolt, the new Khmer Rouge had grown to sufficient strength for the revolt to spread, in 1968, to 11 of the 19 provinces in Cambodia.

> *The coup d'état in 1970 brought to power a government, under General Lon Nol, that was more acceptable to the USA. War with Vietnam followed*

The coup d'état in 1970 brought to power a government, under General Lon Nol, that was more acceptable to the USA. War with Vietnam followed. Estimates of the deaths incurred during the war are between 500,000 and 1 million. Bombing and fighting combined to destroy crops, forests, transport systems and factories and led to massive movements of people out of the rural areas into the towns and cities. An estimated three million people, mostly refugees from the fighting zones, had moved into the towns, the majority of them into the capital. Of these most were living in the areas controlled by Lon Nol and had been subsisting on rice supplied by the USA.

On entering Phnom Penh, in April 1975, the Khmer Rouge forced the city's population to migrate to the countryside to work on the land, similar forced evacuations occurring in other towns. There are fierce debates over the reasons behind the evacuations. As with Stalin and forced collectivization, coercive agricultural policies played a part. Khieu Samphan had theorized about them in his doctoral thesis, submitted to the University of Paris in 1959. There were also highly immediate reasons. With agriculture devastated by war and an estimated three million people recently moved into the urban areas and dependent on rice supplied by the USA, the immediate consequence of the capture of Phnom Penh by the Khmer Rouge meant that this supply of rice was at an end.

Renewed economic crisis and innocents as victims

Reports suggested that rice production achieved in November 1975 was exceptionally high and though the figures are open to doubt good harvests may have followed, but the overall picture suggests a disastrous failure of Khmer Rouge economic policies. By 1979, rice production was no more than the equivalent of the food aid received by the Lon Nol government in the year before the Khmer Rouge took power.

Under the Khmer Rouge declining production was blamed on the workers. They fell victim, in large numbers, either as the direct result of the regime's terror or as the consequence of starvation. In ways parallel to the victimization of 'wreckers' and 'kulaks' in the Soviet Union, a significant number of the victims were those who failed to achieve their work quotas or complained of conditions in the cooperatives. The foreign war also provided enemies who fitted within a long tradition of prejudice (Jackson, 1989). By mid 1978, anti-Vietnamese rhetoric formed a major part of both government and party propaganda and Pol Pot and his associates made endless references to Cambodia's former glory during the Angkor Empire

(800–1444) and promised frequently, and euphemistically, to 'liberate' the ethnic Khmers of Vietnam and Thailand.

Conclusion

In totalitarian regimes, deliberate large-scale killing of innocents is carried out in concealment behind the state façade

In totalitarian regimes, deliberate large-scale killing of innocents is carried out in concealment behind the state façade, the true horror of the regime only to be revealed after its fall. These regimes are very rare, but state terrorism, which is carried out through the state, is far more common and appears in a variety of forms.

Recommended reading

For expansion on these three cases and further arguments, see Rosemary H.T. O'Kane, *Terror, Force and States: The Path From Modernity* (Cheltenham: Edward Elgar, 1996). For further reading on Hannah Arendt, see Margaret Canovan, *Hannah Arendt: A Reinterpretation of her Political Thought* (Cambridge: Cambridge University Press, 1992). Among a large number of works on the individual cases, the following are especially recommended:

Stalin's Soviet Union: Robert Conquest, *The Great Terror: Stalin's Purge of the Thirties* (Harmondsworth: Penguin, 1971); J. Arch Getty and Roberta T. Manning, eds, *Stalinist Terror: New Perspectives* (Cambridge: Cambridge University Press, 1993); Moshe Lewin, *Russian Peasants and Soviet Power: A Study of*

Collectivization (London: George Allen and Unwin, 1967); Edwin Bacon, *The Gulag at War: Stalin's Forced Labour System in the Light of the Archives* (London: Macmillan, 1994).

Nazi Germany: Michael Balfour, *Germany: The Tides of Power* (London: Routledge, 1992); H.B. Krausnick, H. Buchheim, M. Broszat and H.-A. Jacobsen, eds, *Anatomy of the SS State* (London: Collins, 1968); Michael Burleigh and Wolfgang Wippermann, *The Racial State: Germany 1933–1945* (Cambridge: Cambridge University Press, 1991); Norbert Frei, *National Socialist Rule in Germany: The Führer State, 1933–1945* (Oxford: Blackwell, 1993); Ronnie S. Landau, *The Nazi Holocaust* (London: I.B. Taurus, 1992).

Pol Pot's Cambodia: Karl D. Jackson, ed., *Cambodia 1975–1978: Rendezvous with Death* (Princeton, NJ: Princeton University Press, 1989); Ben Kiernan, *The Pol Pot Regime: Race, Power, and Genocide in Cambodia under the Khmer Rouge, 1975–79* (New Haven, CT: Yale University Press, 1996); Michael Vickery, *Cambodia, 1975–1982* (London: Allen and Unwin, 1985); M. Wright, ed., *Cambodia: A Matter of Survival* (Harlow, UK: Longman, 1989).

CHAPTER 5

State terrorism
at home and abroad

THE MASSACRE OF INNOCENTS, the condoning of death squads and vigilante groups, the sponsorship of the terrorism of other regimes or of foreign terrorist groups operating abroad or, simply, carrying out terrorism in foreign countries: these can all be forms of state terrorism. Although differing in so many ways, what these various kinds of state terrorism have, crucially, in common is the abandonment of the due process of law for the adoption of summary justice, under which guilt is assumed and no defence or appeal is allowed. It is this lawlessness that they share with revolutionary reigns of terror and totalitarian regimes. How they differ from those regimes is that they are carried out by ordinary state coercive forces rather than by state forces specially constructed for a system of terror. They also differ in that in these forms state terrorism is likely to be short-lived or confined to some regions only, and, obviously, differ from terror regimes when carried out not at home but abroad.

In contrast to terror regimes, which are rare, the cases of state terrorism are too numerous to cover. The cases discussed are chosen for being illustrative of their type, for being the better documented and for being among the more startling. There is no surprise, therefore, that Rwanda, where one of the worst examples of state terrorism occurred, is the first example.

Massacres and genocidal campaigns

Rwanda, 1994

In Rwanda, in 1994, a section of the population, men, women and also children, took up arms in support of the army and police and engaged in state-sponsored mass murder. Out of a population of approximately eight million people, around half a million were massacred, innocent men, women and children alike, in a 'genocidal campaign' (Melson, 2003).

> *Out of a population of approximately eight million people, around half a million were massacred, innocent men, women and children alike, in a 'genocidal campaign'*

Directed against the Tutsis, the genocidal campaign was led by a radical Hutu grouping; at the centre of government, it called itself 'Hutu Power'. This elite Hutu group was closely linked to President Habyarimana and also to the army, the police, the mass media and the MRND (National Revolutionary Movement for Development), which had been the party of government since 1973.

The mass murder started in the capital, Kigali, and spread throughout Rwanda. The media was used as a propaganda weapon against the Tutsi minority, labelling them as 'traitors' and 'cockroaches', and also against the Hutu opposition to the MRND. Hutu Power's media campaign against the Tutsis, which had first begun in late 1990 and then became accompanied by violence against local Rwandan Tutsis in demonstration of the message, was used to mobilize ordinary civilians into carrying out the slaughter, euphemistically referred to as *umuganda*, meaning communal work. Though far from involving every Hutu, certainly tens of thousands of ordinary Hutu people, wielding machetes, clubs and farming implements, attacked their innocent Tutsi neighbours. In addition to the half a million or so Tutsi victims, Hutus opposed to the MRND were also massacred.

The immediate cause of the massacres was the assassination of President Habyarimana on 6 April 1994. The plane in which he was travelling back from Zambia was shot down, killing everyone on board. The underlying causes of the event, however, went back a long way. An intense cleavage between Hutu and Tutsi in Rwanda had been created under German then Belgium colonialism by Tutsis being given both power and privileges denied to Hutus. In 1959, the cleavage was deepened further, but the domination reversed, when the Hutus overthrew the Tutsi elite. The result ensured a Hutu government on Rwanda's independence in 1962.

Two years after independence there were over a third of a million Tutsi refugees in the neighbouring countries of Burundi and Uganda – and this out of Rwanda's total population of seven million, of which 85 per cent were Hutu. These refugees formed guerrilla forces, which attacked Rwanda at various times, leading to a spiral of further Hutu attacks on Tutsis who had remained in Rwanda. In October 1990 the guerrilla force in Uganda, the Rwandan Patriotic Front (RPF), began an invasion. It was after this that Hutu Power's media campaign against the Tutsis started, spreading the message of the league between the RPF and all Tutsis, both at home and abroad. President Habyarimana was returning from peace talks with the RPF, held in Zambia, when his plane was shot down.

> *Similar massacres to those in Rwanda in 1994 had occurred earlier in Burundi, though there it was not Hutus but Tutsis carrying out the killing*

Similar massacres to those in Rwanda in 1994 had occurred earlier in Burundi, though there it was not Hutus but Tutsis carrying out the killing. In 1972, out of a population of five million, an estimated 100,000 Hutus were massacred by the Tutsi-dominated army. With the number of victims as a proportion of Burundi's population considerably smaller than in the case of Rwanda and the ratio between the population of Hutu and Tutsi in Burundi more equal, the events in Burundi, though clearly a case of state terrorism, did not amount to genocide. One of the most debated cases as genocide are the Armenian massacres of 1915–1916.

Armenia, 1915–16

The massacres took place within the Ottoman Empire (Turkey); in the years 1915 and 1916, between a half and one million innocent Armenians – Kurds – were killed or perished from exposure or disease in concentration camps or in the desert following deportation. In all, it is estimated that the total of victims approximated half of the Armenian population. The reason that there are disputes over the accuracy of the description of these events as genocide is because of doubt over whether the ruling Turkish government ordered extermination. Deportation was ordered but it was not a new strategy, having been used often in the previous century. In the context of the First World War with Russia and Turkey on opposite sides and Anatolia, where most of the Kurds lived, crossing the border between the two countries, concerns about loyalties may have applied, but the treatment of the Armenians went far beyond this. Children were massacred alongside adults; the adults, themselves unarmed innocents, were killed because of their ethnic difference. Similar events to those in Armenia also occurred in Iraq under Saddam Hussein.

Iraq under Saddam Hussein

Saddam Hussein, 1937–2006

Born in Al-Auja, near Takrit, in 1937, into a Sunni Muslim family, Saddam (which means 'Clasher') became attracted to Nazi principles and thence to the ideas of the Ba'ath nationalist movement. Established in Syria in 1943, the movement's ideology was a mixture of Italian Fascism and German National Socialism for 'The Arab Nation'. During the time that the Ba'ath party was in power for the brief spell between two coups d'état in 1963, Saddam began to create the Jihaz Haneen, which he headed. Jihaz Haneen was a secret security organization modelled on the Nazi SS. In July 1968 the Ba'ath party seized power for a second time and Saddam became a member of the ruling Revolutionary Command Council, given responsibility for security, and then became the Deputy Secretary-General.

Purges were carried out in 1968 and 1969 against political activists and Jews. The Shia Islamic leadership became the next target and then, following the outbreak of hostilities in Kurdistan in 1969, the Kurds.

In 1979, Saddam Hussein staged a coup, declared himself president and then carried out a bloody purge of the party. From that point his propaganda machine portrayed him as the 'Father' of the nation with Iraq superior within the pan-Arab nation. He was overthrown in 2003, following the US-led invasion of Iraq; Baghdad fell in April, and he was finally captured in December in his home town. After a lengthy trial for crimes against humanity, he was hanged on 30 December 2006.

Between 1987 and 1989 an estimated 180,000 Kurds were killed and hundreds of thousands more deported from northern Iraq, their villages also being destroyed. The areas where Kurds were living were bombed and attacked with chemical weapons. The worst of all the incidents occurred in a nerve gas attack against the Kurdish town of Halabja, following a Kurdish revolt: an estimated 6,000 people were killed. Similar methods were again used, in 1991, to put down the Kurdish uprising that began after the defeat of Iraq's army following its invasion of Kuwait. In consequence, around 1.5 million Kurds fled Iraq to become refugees in Iran and Turkey.

Yugoslavia under Slobodan Milosovic

For the purposes of what became termed 'ethnic cleansing', massacres also took place in the former Yugoslavia. Following Slobodan Milosovic's election, in December 1990, the country disintegrated into civil war and massacres were carried out in

Bosnia and then Kosovo. They had a similar pattern: first the Serbian army bombed the village and encircled it; then paramilitary forces took over, helped by Serbian civilians from the surrounding areas. Through the encirclement the atrocities carried out within the village against innocent children, women and men took place in secrecy and were conducted with impunity. The largest massacre took place in Srebrenica on 13–15 July 1995, when an estimated 7,000 civilians were killed. Concentration camps in which more atrocities took place were also set up in Bosnia-Herzegovina.

General observations

Ethnic differences have featured in all of these examples – Rwanda, Burundi, Armenia, Iraq, former Yugoslavia – but cleavages based on ethnic or racial differences are also a feature of large numbers of countries where terrorism is not found. It cannot be the case, therefore, that ethnic or racial differences lead, generally, to state terrorism. Rather, the lesson, as for terror regimes, is that governments can choose to exploit prejudices in order to strengthen domination. As the cases have shown, not only ethnic or racial groups but also political opposition may be targeted, defined ever more widely and indiscriminately. As the following examples show, military regimes are common cases of state terrorism and they target political opposition, whether with or without an ethnic dimension, as their victims. Military regimes recently installed by a coup d'état are common perpetrators of state terrorism. In the most shocking cases they operate in league with death squads.

Death squads and disappearances

Indonesia, 1965, and East Timor, 1975–99

In Indonesia in 1965, after General Suharto overthrew President Sukarno in a coup d'état, an estimated one million of the around 120 million population were killed in the space of just a few months. This estimate includes both official and unofficial deaths. In addition, 80,000 people were imprisoned without trial.

> *In Indonesia in 1965, after General Suharto overthrew President Sukarno in a coup d'état, an estimated one million of the around 120 million population were killed in the space of just a few months*

Sukarno had been sympathetic to the Communist Party, PKI. After the military coup anyone suspected of left-wing sympathies was killed or arrested and local communities were encouraged to 'cleanse' themselves of such dangerous political elements. Often the term 'communist' was simply given to a victim retrospectively. Not only did the military in Indonesia, as in Rwanda, encourage the local communities to participate in the killings through propaganda and threats; they also supported right-wing paramilitary gangs in their violence, including providing them with intelligence. On the island of Bali it is estimated that the violence took a toll of 100,000 lives in just 6 months, some 7–8 per cent of Bali's population. People were simply 'disappeared', eventually to be unearthed from mass graves.

Disappearances became a central feature of the conduct of the Indonesian army following their invasion of East Timor in 1975. At the time, East Timor was a Portuguese colony in the process of moving towards independence. By 1980 East Timor had become what one East Timorese resident of Dili, the capital city, described as 'a world of terror' (Taylor, 2003). The Indonesian soldiers' term for these disappearances was 'gone for a swim' (*mandi laut*), a reference to their disposal through being dumped by helicopters into the sea with weights attached to their feet. The victims included those who took up arms against the army of occupation but the violence was also indiscriminate, used against unarmed, innocent men, women and children.

In East Timor, not only was violence indiscriminate; imprisonment was also arbitrary and indeterminate. There were no trials held until 1984, and then only in Dili. At any point prisoners could be taken out and killed. The use of torture, already widespread, was officially sanctioned in 1982 and its viciousness increased the longer the occupation continued. Forced resettlements into camps were carried out and each camp was under harsh control with severe restrictions of movement beyond them. By 1990 nearly all East Timorese were living in the camps, which also served a system of forced labour. On the assessment of the Foreign Affairs Committee of the Australian parliament, by 1993 more than 200,000 East Timorese had been killed since 1975, almost a third of the population.

Far from all military governments installed by coups have engaged in state terrorism but one of the most shocking cases, partly because of its previous liberal democratic system, is Chile.

Chile under Pinochet

Salvador Allende's elected government was overthrown by a military coup on 11 September 1973, bringing General Pinochet to power. Vengeance killings of retribution immediately began against anyone, guilty or innocent alike, construed as having supported the previous regime in any way. The new military regime created make-shift prisons out of the two

> *Vengeance killings of retribution immediately began against anyone, guilty or innocent alike, construed as having supported the previous regime in any way*

football stadiums in the capital, Santiago, in which 7,000 prisoners were held at one time and seven execution camps were in operation within days of the coup. In other cities stadiums were used and ships were turned into floating prisons; prison-torture-execution centres were soon established. In the first few months after the coup 15,000 people are estimated to have been killed by the military, shot, tortured or beaten to death. Along with members of Allende's government and its supporters entirely innocent bystanders were grabbed from the streets. A Swedish journalist, who was himself held in the National Stadium in Santiago for a week, reported in a Stockholm daily newspaper in October 1973: 'Almost every morning dead bodies turn up lying along the Avenida Departmental on the outskirts of Santiago. They appear near bus stops, where they can frighten people. Their faces are smashed in with rifle butts so that they are unrecognizable' (quoted in Roxborough *et al.*, 1977: 240). Similar reports were made of Argentina.

Argentina and Triple A

Disappearances became a crucial feature of Argentina in the 1970s and especially during the years following the military coup d'état in March 1976. Estimates of those killed under the rule of the junta, from their coming to power in 1976 to their removal in 1982, range between 10,000 and 30,000 victims. The existence of revolutionary guerrilla movements – the Montoneros and the People's Revolutionary Army (ERP) being the major groups – both provided the background to state terrorism and was used as its justification. The state violence was quite out of proportion to that of the guerrillas. According to the regime's own figures, the guerrillas' victims totalled 700, hardly a match for the tens of thousands killed by the regime. The guerrilla forces are estimated to have numbered only 5,000 at their height, their actions, furthermore, being mostly reactive (Gillespie, 1995).

The Anti-Communist Alliance of Argentina, the Triple A death squad, had been set up by the government before the 1976 coup and Triple A had assassinated around 2,000 people since 1973. But Triple A's role changed after the military junta came to power and began its 'dirty war'; from then on Triple A became more integrated into the covert system. The junta set up 340 secret detention centres for the interrogation and torture of those detained. These centres operated outside of the law. The 'disappeared' victims were buried in mass graves or dropped into the River Plate from aircraft.

Although the torturing of suspects can be carried out by repressive regimes in order to intimidate actual and potential rebels to change their behaviour, in Argentina the junta chose to kill thousands of innocent people. Not only were the unarmed killed just because they may have had some connection with a suspected guerrilla, but those who thought differently were also killed. This included those in the professions such as psychologists and sociologists and also manual labourers who believed in workers' rights, so-called 'troublemakers'.

> *Although the torturing of suspects can be carried out by repressive regimes in order to intimidate actual and potential rebels to change their behaviour, in Argentina the junta chose to kill thousands of innocent people*

Guatemala under Ríos Montt

An even more extreme example is found in Guatemala: out of a total population of 10 million, 200,000 people were killed or 'disappeared' in 1981–83. In the assessment of the Historical Clarification Commission (CEH), administered by the United Nations and published in 1999, the Guatemalan state and its allied death squads were responsible for 93 per cent of the violations (the guerrillas responsible for 3 per cent) and the military engaged in 626 massacres. Furthermore, though the head of government, General Ríos Montt, denied it on the grounds that they were political enemies, the ethnic cleavage, too, seems to have been exploited. The state especially targeted Mayans, the native Guatemalans, in what the report describes as 'acts of genocide'. An ethnic aspect is also found in one of the most shocking African cases.

Uganda under Idi Amin

The military coup occurred in January 1971. Although the evidence does not support the claim that state terrorism was ethnically determined, members of the Muslim Kakwa nationality, of which President Idi Amin was one, together with other Muslim communities, primarily the Nubis, were amongst those most protected from the terrorism. Between 1971 and 1979 out of a population of 13 million people it is estimated that, at a minimum, 12,000 to 30,000 people were killed by the regime, with many estimates putting the figure as high as between 100,000 and 500,000 victims (Kannyo, 2000). Some of these killings were the act of a repressive regime directed at opposition: initially, the main targets were those supportive of the previous Obote regime and therefore opposed to the military coup that had brought Amin to power. The targets, however, changed over time and as the years wore on the killings became increasingly indiscriminate. From the beginning the right to legal representation was mostly disregarded and there is no evidence that any appeals were ever held and punishment was harsh, ranging from death to 15 years in prison even for minor offences. Though set up after the coup as part of the ordinary police force, the Public Safety Unit came to operate as a death squad, dispensing summary justice, including public executions. Other security units, too, acted as death squads and mass killings also occurred.

The crimes perpetrated by Amin's regime have never been investigated fully but El Salvador in the 1980s, where death squads were notorious, has been subject to full investigation and this case proves especially helpful, therefore, in gaining an understanding of death squads.

El Salvador

Mutilated bodies of the tortured would be found, in El Salvador, thrown on to roadsides or tossed into body dumps. Between 9,000 and 10,000 civilians were killed just in 1980, and another 9,000 to 10,000 victims in the first half of 1981, with government forces the major perpetrators. One of the death squads sometimes carved the initials EM (*Escuadrón de la Muerte*, Death Squad) on their victims; another sometimes tucked a piece of paper on the victim declaring the killing done by the General Maximiliano Hernández Martínez Anti-Communist Brigade.

In 1993 a Commission on the Truth for El Salvador, sponsored by the United Nations, concluded that nearly 85 per cent of the cases of summary justice and torture had been carried out by the state, paramilitary groups connected with them and by death squads. The most famous death squad killing was that of Archbishop Romero in 1980. In striking comparison, the Commission also concluded that the FLMN (Farabundo Martí National Liberation Front), the coalition of guerrilla groups that formed in late 1980 in response to the escalating state violence, was responsible for just 5 per cent of the executions.

The Truth Commission also drew attention not only to the encouragement given by the civilian and military authorities to the activities of the death squads but also to their active participation within them. Furthermore, it went so far as not just to comment on the State's concealment of its responsibility but to conclude that it had, in the Commission's words, 'created an atmosphere of complete impunity for the murderers who worked in the squads' (quoted in Arnson, 2000: 89). El Salvador had a history of vigilante groups, both official and private, working in league with the regular army and the paramilitary police forces.

Generalizing on vigilantism

The view of the weakness or inefficiency of the judicial process and its substitution for summary justice is common to death squads and vigilante groups

The view of the weakness or inefficiency of the judicial process and its substitution for summary justice is common to death squads and vigilante groups and not only, as in most of the above examples, in countries where left-wing guerrillas oppose military regimes. Indeed, the most thoroughly researched example began not in the twentieth but the eighteenth century. The case, that of vigilantism in the United States, demonstrates exactly the logic of the rejection of the due process of law for the goal of crime control.

Some prominent people in late nineteenth-century America, including judges, lawyers and political leaders, supported vigilantism and lynch law because they believed that it dealt more efficiently and more effectively with crime. The argument was made not only that vigilante groups and lynch law dealt with crime more quickly – it was argued, for example, that appeals made the due process of law slow – but also that they saved the taxpayer money. A figure saved as high as 20 thousand dollars for bringing a murderer to trial, conviction and execution was claimed in a law journal of 1892. A newspaper report on public opinion on lynchings in Golden, Colorado, in 1879 concluded that 'on every side the popular verdict seemed to be that the hanging was not only well merited, but a positive gain to the county, saving it at least five or six thousand dollars' (quoted in Brown, 1971: 111).

Vigilantism as a large-scale movement began in South Carolina in 1767–69. Lynch law, so named after the colonel who first used it, began in 1779 in Virginia during the American War of Independence. After the revolution both vigilante movements and lynch law spread. The first Ku Klux Klan movement was one of these: the Klan of the Reconstruction. There were also thousands of other lynch mobs nationwide but especially in the south, where African Americans were by far the most common victims and likely to be subject to torture before being killed. It is estimated that between 1767 and 1951 around 6,000 people were executed either by vigilantes or by lynch mobs. Between 1883 and 1898 the total of those executed illegally far exceeded the total of those executed legally.

While some individuals, including even some of the highest judges and politicians, made arguments at times in support of vigilantism or lynch law, complicity with lynchings, whippings and the like took place at the local, not national, level. Local lawyers and judges, sheriffs, police and gaolers might be complicit, passively looking the other way and sometimes actively taking part. For them controlling crime, punishing the individual as quickly as possible, was more important than the process of law and this attitude was justified by its supporters not only in terms of saving time and money but also in terms of its serving what the local people wanted. Justified, indeed, as serving 'popular sovereignty', an argument used in support of democracy itself, no less. In a similar mind-set, in the Philippines in the late 1980s vigilante groups joined in the mobilization for free elections with calls to 'Kill for Peace! Kill for Democracy!' (Alsa Masa Checkpoint Slogan, Davao, the Philippines, 1987).

Crime-control vigilantism can occur wherever groups determined to defend the status quo (always so defined to preserve their own beneficial position within it) believe that the government is considered insufficiently effectual in its defence. The equivalent can also occur in the sponsorship of state terrorism abroad and here, too, the United States provides examples.

International state terrorism

United States

The United Nations-administered Historical Clarification Commission report on Guatemala 1981–83, published in 1999, not only condemned the Guatemalan political and military authorities but also condemned the United States for providing the Guatemalan security forces with financial, technical and material support. In Chile, the United States was involved in moves to undermine and overthrow Allende's Popular Unity government. The US government also allocated, at a minimum, seven million dollars to the CIA, the US Central Intelligence Agency, for support of those opposed to Allende. Some of this money together with CIA assistance went to right-wing paramilitary groups in Chile, such as *Patria y Libertad* (Fatherland and Liberty). In a direct transfer of state terrorism abroad, the Argentinian death squad Triple A

> *In Chile, the United States was involved in moves to undermine and overthrow Allende's Popular Unity government*

assassinated General Prats when he was in Buenos Aires. Prats supported Allende's government as legitimate and therefore needed to be removed for Pinochet's takeover.

The US government classified the Allende government as Marxist and, in the assessment of the American government, therefore communist and, as such, guilty of being opposed to democracy. Viewed as guilty, action taken against Allende's government was considered justified. In practice, rather than being communist, Allende's Popular Unity (Unidad Popular) was a coalition of parties, which included the Communist Party, socialist parties and also liberal parties. Not only was Allende and his government democratically elected, with free and fair elections in which multiple parties competed, but his government abided by the constitution and introduced legislation through the Congress and continued to have elections with competing political parties and introduced universal suffrage.

More recently, in Nicaragua, the CIA played a major part in the Contra War against the Sandinista government, which came to power in the revolution of 1979. In February 1982, the *Washington Post* reported that the CIA had been given a budget of US$19 million to undertake covert action against Nicaragua. Funding and assistance continued through to 1989. Yet, in June 1986, the International Court of Justice at The Hague ruled that by interfering in the internal affairs of Nicaragua the USA had been in breach of international law. And when, in February 1988, the US Congress rejected President Reagan's request for more funds for the Contras, funds were procured for them through the covert selling of arms to Iran in what became known as the 'Iran–Contra Affair'. These events took place even though the Sandinistas were elected to power through a process of multi-party competition and universal suffrage in 1984 and these elections were judged as free and fair by all independent observers (with the singular exception of those from the United States).

In these cases, the USA has shown itself more concerned with fighting the 'crime' of communism, Marxism, socialism or whatever term might be applied to behaviour not in accordance with their interpretation of democracy (one incorporating free market capitalism, the status quo from which they gain benefit) than with following the due process of law. The USA has, thereby, been implicated in supporting acts, directly or indirectly, that have led to the death, torture and suffering of innocent people. The USA has not, of course, been the only country involved in this kind of international state terrorism and far worse examples are to be found elsewhere. Furthermore, it is important to recognize that one of the reasons why it is possible to piece together US actions and why, therefore, criticism of the United States is well voiced is because, ironically, the USA is an open society with freedom of information. For other cases, the more closed nature of their governments and societies requires piecing together more speculative evidence.

The Soviet Union and the communist network

During the Cold War, which developed after the Second World War and took definite shape in 1949 when Germany split into East and West, a view formed in the United States that there was a communist network of terrorism. The argument went that, from the mid-1960s, the Communist Bloc countries began to infiltrate left-wing terrorist movements throughout the world and set up special training schools in Czechoslovakia, Cuba and

East Germany. Palestinians who trained in the Cuban camp then, it was claimed, set up their own *fedayeen* training camps with Cuban instructors and were also trained in and armed by the Soviet Union. The Soviet Union was believed to be turning out 'other professional terrorists by the thousands – European, South and North American, African, Asian – inside Russia or in

The Soviet Union was believed to be turning out 'other professional terrorists by the thousands'

the satellite states of Czechoslovakia, East Germany, Hungary, Bulgaria, North Korea, South Yemen' (Stirling 1981: 15). Furthermore, not only Soviet arms but also Libyan money were implicated in the network of terrorist groups, which included, among others, Middle East groups, the IRA, ETA, the Italian Red Brigades and the German Red Army Faction (RAF). Questions were raised at the time over the compatibility of the goals of these various groups for coordinated action and the observation was also made that it was at least as likely that some groups, the IRA for one, was 'using' the Soviet Union rather than the other way around.

From the mid-1980s a loosening took place in the Soviet Union under Gorbachev, the era of *glasnost* and *perestroika*, and a clear picture began to emerge. The training camp at Balashika near Moscow connected with, mainly Arab, terrorist training was closed and relations with terrorist groups, such as they were, ended. Since the fall of communism in Eastern Europe and the opening of archives it has, also, become clear that the East German secret police, the Stasi, aided the Red Army Faction in West Germany and gave support to significant terrorist individuals, such as Carlos the Jackal who chose to base himself in East Berlin. The Stasi also collected intelligence on Palestinian groups and on others, including the IRA, ETA and the Italian Red Brigades, though for what purpose is not clear. The evidence does not support the claim that East Germany shared information with the other Eastern Bloc countries, nor even with the KGB. There is evidence of Stasi help in just two terrorist attacks, both carried out in Berlin. One of these was the bombing of La Belle discotheque in April 1986 for which a German court later established that the bombings were carried out by a Palestinian with explosives and logistic support provided by the two officials of the Libyan legation in East Berlin.

Libya

Following Colonel Gaddafi's coup d'état in 1969, Libya gave support to a variety of terrorist groups, mostly Arab ones, but groups were also supported in central and west Africa. Gaddafi then went on to assist the German Red Army Faction and the Palestinian group Black September. More details of these groups are in the chapters to come. There were unconfirmed reports of camps in Libya for training foreign terrorists in the 1980s (up to 8,000 being trained a year) and that some Palestinian groups received huge sums of money from Libya. Gaddafi, however, changed favours and support could not be relied upon.

In Europe, Libyan terrorists were implicated in the December 1985 attacks on the Israeli airline, El Al, ticket counters at the airports in Vienna and Rome as well as the April 1986 bomb attack on the discotheque in West Berlin. Following that bombing, in which two American servicemen were killed and

79 people were injured, the United States launched an air attack on Libya. In the raid, which crossed Gaddafi's imaginary 'line of death' across the Gulf, 93 Libyan civilians were killed. From then on claims of Libyan involvement in terrorism fell. In December 1988, however, the bombing of a Pan Am passenger aeroplane over Lockerbie, Scotland, which killed all 259 people on board, was blamed on Libya. It led to the eventual arrest of two Libyans, one of whom was found guilty, though Gaddafi has continued to deny state responsibility.

Although Libya supported Arab terrorist groups over the years this support was political, not religious. It was the Iranian Revolution of 1979 that made the difference.

Iran

Iranian Islamic revolutionary guards were sent to Lebanon in June 1982, following the Israeli invasion. Initially joining with Syrian and Lebanese forces in their fight against the Israelis, the Islamic Revolutionary Guards established headquarters in Baal-beck in the Bekaa Valley where they received orders from the secret 'War against Satan Committee' of the Iranian Islamic Republic. The aim of the committee was to use the Lebanese Shiite groups of the Islamic Jihad movement, which included the Hizbollah, a terrorist group created and sponsored by Iran in 1982, in terrorist operations against Western and, especially, American presence. The size of the Islamic Jihad was estimated in the mid-1980s, to include between 500 and 1,000 Iranian Revolutionary Guards on top of the several hundred Lebanese Shiites, with training and weapons supplied by Iran and forces also channelled in through Syria. Islamic Jihad declared responsibility for having carried out the bombing of the French Embassy in Beirut in May 1982 and, in April 1983, for the attack on the US embassy in Beirut in which a suicide lorry-bomb killed 63 people and injured a further 120 people.

Following the death of Ayatollah Khomeini in 1989 and the Taif Accord, which brought peace to Lebanon, Hizbollah turned to participation in the Lebanese elections and support for Islamic Jihad and Hamas (Islamic Resistance Movement), Palestinian groups based within the West Bank and Gaza Strip. Iran assists Hamas financially, estimated at tens of millions of dollars, and also gives military training and logistical support (Abu-Amr, 1994). More directly, Iranian terrorists attacked a Jewish community centre in Buenos Aires, Argentina, in July 1994, killing 85 people and injuring more than 200. The incident led to Iranian diplomats being expelled.

There are many other examples of links between terrorist groups and foreign countries, such as Syria, Iraq and Sudan. To understand such links more fully, it is necessary to turn away from state terrorism, in its variety of forms, to consider the terrorism carried out by terrorist groups formed within society and to do so by beginning not with international but with domestic terrorism.

Recommended reading

On cases of massacre and genocide excellent, concise contributions can be found in Robert Gellately and Ben Kiernan, eds, *The Specter of Genocide: Mass Murder in Historical Perspective* (Cambridge and New York: Cambridge University Press, 2003). Similarly excellent case studies on death squads can be found in Bruce B. Campbell and Arthur D. Brenner, eds, *Death Squads in Global Perspective: Murder with Deniability* (London: Macmillan, 2000). On Saddam Hussein, see Adel Darwish and Gregory Alexander, *Unholy Babylon: The Secret History of Saddam's War* (London: Victor Gollancz, 1991).

On international state terrorism, see especially the chapter by Grant Wardlaw, 'Terror as an Instrument of Foreign Policy', in David C. Rapoport, ed., *Inside Terrorist Organizations* (London: Frank Cass, 2001), and the chapter by Michael Stohl, 'States, Terrorism and State Terrorism: The Role of the Superpowers', in Robert O. Slater and Michael Stohl, eds, *Current Perspectives on International Terrorism* (London: Macmillan, 1988). See also Walter Laqueur, *The New Terrorism: Fanaticism and the Arms of Mass Destruction* (London: Phoenix Press, 2001) and Raymond Tanter, *Rogue Regimes: Terrorism and Proliferation* (London: Macmillan, 1999).

Keesing's Contemporary Archives to 1987 (London and Harlow: Keesing's Publications, Longman), re-named *Keesing's Record of World Events* from 1988 (Cambridge: Keesing's Worldwide), is an excellent primary source for the examples.

CHAPTER 6

Terrorist groups from within liberal democracies

WHY GROUPS MIGHT WANT TO form to undertake terrorist acts against repressive dictatorships and terror regimes is easy to imagine. Without means for political participation, and without the protections afforded by a legal system in which guilt and innocence are meaningful, and through which human rights are protected, to engage in mass protests would be to take huge risks. In such circumstances there would be obvious advantages in keeping opposition clandestine and the use of terror would be in keeping with the violent nature of the regime. In liberal democracies, however, quite opposite conditions apply: there are legal means for changing governments in which free and fair elections play an important part; there are legitimate opportunities for expression of opinions and for active participation; and there is legal protection for protest – strikes, demonstrations and the like. It follows that there are no simple answers as to why terrorist groups develop within liberal democracies.

One way of developing understanding is to focus on the openness of liberal democratic societies. While repressive dictatorships and terror

One way of developing understanding is to focus on the openness of liberal democratic societies

regimes may provide more justification for clandestine violent opposition groups, the brutal nature of those regimes and the closed nature of the societies over which they rule mitigate against the operation of terrorist groups. In contrast, while justification for terrorism in democracies is hard to conceive, the very openness of democratic societies makes the operation of terrorist groups more feasible. The freedom of association that is characteristic of democratic societies facilitates the development and organization of terrorist groups. Freedom of speech and most especially of the media play into the terrorists' hands, providing the means to publicize their acts and even aiding their coordination.

To suggest that in having open societies and less violent, more responsive, more representative governments, constrained by laws, democracy is itself a facilitating condition for terrorism does not, however, explain why terrorists should want to attack democratically elected governments. The most obvious answer would be that they reject democracy either in theory or in the reality of the form currently experienced. Ideology may be involved in this, as for example in the rejection of bourgeois democracy, so clearly voiced by the anarchist Emile Henry in France in 1894, or in the modern-day Marxist's anti-capitalism or the fascists' rejection of liberalism and pluralism.

Ideology is not, however, necessarily involved in acts of terror: motivations may be bound up simply with the would-be terrorists' contorted outlook, which may, at most, have only tenuous links with wider ideas or, indeed, with a wider organization. One such example is the Oklahoma City bombing, carried out on 19 April 1995, in which 169 people were killed and more than 500 others were injured. Yet Timothy McVeigh who carried out the bombing was not part of a terrorist organization. He had an association with right-wing militias and held a belief that the US government interfered too much in citizens' lives, but the specific trigger to his actions was the anniversary of the end of the federal government's siege on the Branch Davidian compound at Waco, Texas, in 1993. It had left 80 people dead.

Although the Oklahoma City bombing was a dramatic example of a terrorist attack, being the act of an individual and with the motivations specific it is not a case from which general lessons on terrorist groups can be produced. It is the more durable terrorist organizations from which general lessons can be drawn. Four such groups stand out: the Irish Republican Army (IRA)/ Provisional Irish Republican Army (PIRA) in Northern Ireland; the Basque Separatists (ETA) in Spain; the Red Army Faction (RAF, also known as the Baader–Meinhof Gang or Group) in Germany; and the Red Brigades in Italy.

The IRA/PIRA has by far the longest history of the four groups and it also has the highest incidence of attacks and killings. It is estimated that just between 1950 and 1995 the IRA/PIRA carried out 1,369 attacks resulting in a total of 602 killings. As a comparison, ETA, from 1967 to 1995, carried out 374 attacks leading to a total of 447 killings; the Red Brigades, from 1972 to 1988, made 59 attacks producing a total of 48 killings; and the Red Army Faction, from 1968 to 1993, made 106 attacks resulting in 31 killings (Engene, 2004).

IRA/PIRA

The IRA first made an appearance, as a militia called the Irish Volunteers, in the Easter Rising of 1916, the failed attempt to separate Ireland from British rule. It was renamed the Irish Republican Army (IRA, *Óglaigh na h-Éireann*) in 1919, during the

The IRA first made an appearance, as a militia called the Irish Volunteers in the Easter Rising of 1916, the failed attempt to separate Ireland from British rule

War of Independence, which was fought from 1919 to 1921. In January 1922 the Dublin parliament voted to accept an agreement under which Ireland became the Irish Free State with the exception of six of the nine counties of the northern province of Ulster. These six counties were to have a separate parliament (Stormont) and remain under British rule as part of the United Kingdom of Great Britain and Northern Ireland. The IRA refused to accept the agreement and a civil war ensued from 1922–23, the IRA operating as a guerrilla army. Defeated by the Free State forces, the IRA regrouped, as a secret society bound by oath, to continue its violent campaign for a united Irish Republic. Brutality characterized many of the acts in Ireland but it was in 1939 that the clear move to terrorist tactics occurred with a bombing campaign in the cities of mainland Britain. The first deaths resulted in August when an IRA bomb exploded in Coventry city centre killing five people and injuring many more. The campaign continued until 1945. A new campaign, of sabotage, began in 1956; waged across the border into Northern Ireland it petered out after six years, leaving the IRA both in disarray and as a discredited nationalist force.

Events then took a new turn. A separate civil rights movement campaigning peacefully for the same rights to apply in Northern Ireland as for all British citizens developed. The failure of the Republicans to achieve a united Ireland had been compounded by the re-drawing of Ulster as only six counties, which ensured a Protestant majority in Northern Ireland. The electoral system, which was changed from proportional representation to a first-past-the-post system, then added to the problem. In the Stormont elections the Unionist Party, the loyalist party supported by Protestants, generally won around three-quarters of the seats with just over half of the votes. This situation was also mirrored in local elections. In Derry/Londonderry city, evidence of gerrymandering was most striking in having a Unionist majority on the Council in spite of a majority of the population being Catholic and nationalist. It was to redress these democratic shortcomings – no alteration in office, with the Unionists always the winners, and the minority rights of Catholics not being fully represented – that led to the development of the civil rights campaign. It provoked a backlash from Protestant militants. This together with the government using unexpectedly harsh force against peaceful protest led to the resuscitation of the IRA.

The civil rights movement expanded rapidly and, on 16 November 1968, in Derry/Londonderry, 15,000 people took part in a civil rights march. As support for the civil rights movement grew, the protests spread, and the cleavage between the two sides – Catholics/Nationalists and Protestants/Loyalists – became more intense. Political grievances were reinforced by economic differences. Compared with Protestant men, Catholic men were nearly two-and-a-half times as likely to be unemployed. Protestants were also more likely to be employed in non-manual jobs and especially in professional and managerial occupations. In general, Protestants benefited more in their overall living standards as compared with Catholics.

As the political violence increased, the police, the Royal Ulster Constabulary (RUC), showed themselves unable, or unwilling, to protect the civil rights protestors. On 12 August 1969 rioting escalated and barricades were erected in Bogside, a Nationalist area

As the political violence increased, the police, the Royal Ulster Constabulary (RUC), showed themselves unable, or unwilling, to protect the civil rights protestors

in Derry/Londonderry. Rioting then broke out elsewhere and on 14 August six people were shot and killed in battles in Belfast. The B-Specials, an auxiliary police force comprised mainly of Protestants, 'went on a spree of shooting and arson .... The spectacle of Bombay Street, between the Protestant Shankill and Catholic Falls Roads, burning from end to end' (Brian Mawhinney, future Conservative Party politician in Northern Ireland, quoted in English, 2004: 108). With civil war threatening, the British army arrived the next day, given the job of peacekeeping.

The split between the Provisional IRA (PIRA) and what became known as the Official IRA (OIRA) took place in December 1969. It occurred over the issue of whether a predominantly military or predominantly political approach would be taken to defending Catholics in Northern Ireland in the event of another

August 1969. A breakaway group from Sinn Feín, the political wing of the IRA, soon joined them and, with no more than a few hundred members of the PIRA in early 1970, insensitive handling of the situation in Northern Ireland by the British government brought new recruits.

In January 1971 the use of guns for sniping at soldiers, violence used against armed representatives of the British state, was supplemented by a new strategy – a bombing campaign. OIRA rejected this use of terrorist tactics. By the summer explosions of one or more bombs were happening every day. On 9 August 1971, internment – the holding of suspects without trial under the Special Powers Act of 1922 – began. From that point the PIRA's bombing campaign escalated. As the violence grew, both recruitment and support for the group expanded further. In Derry/Londonderry city, on 30 January 1972, British soldiers opened fire on a protest march against internment, killing 13 unarmed protestors. These events, which became known as 'Bloody Sunday', led to the PIRA heightening its car-bombing campaign. It also led to the abolition of the Stormont government.

In sharp contrast, the Official IRA declared a ceasefire in 1972, reducing its military capacity to become a completely political organization by the late 1970s. Those within the OIRA who disagreed with the move from a military capacity and who wanted to retain use of force formed the Irish National Liberation Army (INLA) and specialized in the assassination of prominent individuals. Loyalist paramilitary organizations – the Ulster Freedom Fighters (UFF) and the Ulster Volunteer Force (UVF) – also carried out attacks and killings. Between 1969 to 1998, more than 15,000 bomb explosions occurred in the conflict. Beginning in 1973, IRA bombing campaigns were also carried out in mainland Britain.

Terrorism in Northern Ireland developed against a background of underlying social economic and political grievances, which, in effect, blocked the participation of the Catholic section of the population. Their grievances were intensified by the initially peaceful civil rights protests, which sought to remedy

Terrorism in Northern Ireland developed against a background of underlying social economic and political grievances, which, in effect, blocked the participation of the Catholic section of the population

the problem of unequal participation, being met by the heavy use of force by the government. As the case of the PIRA has shown, however, the adoption of terrorist tactics did not inevitably follow: their adoption was a choice, one that others and, not least, the OIRA, even when suffering the same problems and even when part of the same violent group, rejected. That the relationship between grievances and terrorism is far from simple is also strikingly evident in the case of the Basque Separatists, in Spain: ETA has continued in spite of the significant change from the Franco dictatorship to post-Franco democracy.

ETA

Euskadi 'ta Askatasuna (ETA, Basque Homeland and Freedom) was founded in 1959 by some ten or so militant members of the youth organization of the Basque Nationalist Party, PNV.

From its founding, ETA has sought not only the regeneration of Basque language and culture but also Basque independence and has sought to achieve it through the use of arms. The early strategy of guerrilla warfare proved impractical against the strong repressive forces of Franco's dictatorship and in 1964 ETA changed its organization to that of a secret army. The decision to engage in armed resistance was a logical step against the violent and repressive Spanish state under Franco, which declared 12 'states of exception' between 1956 and 1975. These declarations in effect introduced martial law to some or all regions of Spain. Five of the declarations applied to the whole of Spain, including therefore the Basque Country; six of them were directed solely to Basque provinces.

The effect of the states of exception in the Basque provinces was not only to substitute government with violence but also to heighten identity with a Basque nation, distinct from the Spanish nation. It was this nationalism, the goal of independence, that ETA used to continue to justify their use of terrorist tactics against the parliamentary democracy that was set up after Franco, who died in 1975. In 1974, when Franco's health was failing, a division occurred in ETA similar to that within the IRA in 1969–70. ETA divided into ETA-M (or ETA-Militar), a group supporting purely military action, and ETA-PM (or ETA-Político-Militar), supporting a combination of political and military action.

Over time, ETA-PM, like the OIRA in Northern Ireland, increasingly favoured participation in the democratic process. The first elections in Spain after Franco's death took place in 1977. While ETA-PM disintegrated and then disbanded, ETA-M continued, bolstered by memories of the central Spanish state's violent behaviour and the heroism of those who had fought against it. The wider support of the Basque Movement for National Liberation (MLNV) also continued and it organized marches against repressive actions taken by the state, especially in respect of imprisoned ETA members (Llera *et al.*, 1993). One of ETA-M's specialities became exploding bombs on tourist beaches.

New Left terrorism

In contrast to both the IRA and ETA, neither the development of the Red Army Faction (RAF) in Germany nor that of the Red Brigades in Italy was linked to the past through a national movement. Rather, they were left-wing terrorist groups that developed from a new social movement, principally based on radical student movements: the New Left of the post-war generation. The New Left rejected current liberal democracies as a sham but supported ideals of democracy that were truly participatory and truly social democratic. Similar radical student movements were common throughout liberal democracies in the late 1960s and early 1970s, with protests focused around opposition to the Vietnam War, but it was only in Germany and Italy that enduring terrorist groups developed. What stands out as similar between these two cases and different from the others is that in contrast to those liberal democracies of the late 1960s, only Italy and the German Federal Republic shared a history of totalitarianism: fascist totalitarian dictatorship and Nazi totalitarian regime, respectively. Contrasting, therefore, with established democratic systems, the democracies in Germany and Italy were essentially new democracies, set up after 1945, with specific political problems relating to their political pasts.

Red Army Faction

To the New Left in West Germany politics appeared undemocratic. Because of threats from communist East Germany there were some restrictions on civil liberties. The Communist Party, (KPD, *Kommunistische Partei Deutschlands*), like the Nazi Party, was banned, yet some organizations for ex-members of the SS were allowed. There was also a felt lack of public discussion about Germany's responsibility for the Holocaust and the youth of the late 1960s questioned the conduct of their parents' generation and, in consequence, respect for parents and authority was weak. Furthermore, Nazis were not just a thing of the past: there were ex-Nazis holding posts in the civil service, the judiciary, business, the medical profession and even senior positions in government. For example, Federal Chancellor Kiesinger had held a high post in the Propaganda Ministry of the Third Reich. Added to this, there was a rise in votes for the neo-Nazi National Democratic Party (NDP). In contrast to the outlawing of the Communist Party, the attempt to ban the NDP under the constitution had failed and it succeeded in gaining seats in the Land parliaments and came close to doing so in the Reichstag.

In November 1966, a new government was formed as a Grand Coalition: it included the Christian Democrats (CDU) and the Social Democrats (SPD). This was the first time since the Weimar Republic that the SPD had been included in government. Although democratic in the sense of the government being representative of votes cast, the Grand Coalition meant that parliament lacked an opposition. To the New Left this suggested that there was no real debate, no real alternative in German politics and therefore no way of achieving change through the parliamentary system. So, students took to the streets to protest against what they viewed as authoritarian democracy and they also demonstrated in support of peace and in opposition to the Vietnam War and imperialism. In response to the protests the police used tough tactics and demonstrations became violent confrontations. The killing of a demonstrator, Benno Ohnesorg, by the police in a demonstration against the visit of the Shah of Iran in 1967 created a martyr.

The heavy-handed behaviour of the police, much as in Northern Ireland where police responses to the civil rights movement had been harsh, served, likewise, to create a sense of injustice among the demonstrators in Germany. In their minds, the injustice delegitimized the whole state and their anti-state feelings were reinforced by sections of

The heavy-handed behaviour of the police, much as in Northern Ireland where police responses to the civil rights movement had been harsh, served, likewise, to create a sense of injustice among the demonstrators in Germany

the press owned by the right-wing magnate Axel Springer whipping up anti-student views. The demonstrators' anti-state feelings were then hardened by the government amending the constitution – The Basic Law – to extend emergency powers. The violence of the German police actions was taken as proof that the system was turning into a fascist state. The failure to ban the neo-Nazi NDP, in contrast to the outlawed

Communist Party, added to the view. The accusation that the German state was fascist – *Faschisierung* – was crucial to the Red Army Faction, which saw it as a reason to withdraw from open protest.

The first move from violent protest to terrorist action occurred in April 1968 when Andreas Baader and Gudrun Ensslin set fire to two department stores in Frankfurt; their rationale was that the fires conveyed to the German people the feeling of what it would be like to be in Vietnam. The Socialist German Students' Association (SDS) rejected the move to arson as 'unjustifiable acts of terrorism' and dissociated itself from the terrorist group. The last mass battle with the police was in early November 1968 from which point the student movement began to disintegrate. In early 1970, the new Brandt (SPD) administration (a Social Democrat and Free Democrat (SDP–FDP) coalition) called an amnesty on mass demonstrators and induced them to work 'inside the system' (quoted in Merkl, 1995). Terrorist attacks, against high profile targets such as US bases and the Axel Springer press building in Hamburg, however, continued.

The Red Army Faction (*Rote Armée Fraktion*) was founded as an organized group in May 1970 by Ulrike Meinhof and Horst Mahler; in the media they remained dubbed the Baader–Meinhof Group or Gang.

Andreas Baader, 1947–77, and Ulrike Meinhof, 1934–76

Andreas Baader was born in May 1947 in München. He was not a student and had been in trouble with the police for car and motorcycle theft. He was politicized by his girlfriend Gudrun Ensslin, a student activist in the 1960s, and was attracted to the radical movement by its potential for violence. He was admired within the group as a man of action. Convicted of the department store arson attacks in 1968, Baader and Ensslin served 14 months in prison, were released awaiting their appeal and then escaped to France. Horst Mahler was one of their defence lawyers. Baader was arrested again in 1970 and, in May, was rescued from police custody by an armed gang, which included Gudrun Ensslin and Ulrike Meinhof.

Ulrike Meinhof was born in October 1934 and was married with two children, twin girls. She was the editor of the left-wing student magazine *Konkret*; her husband was its publisher but they divorced in 1968. Following the armed rescue of Baader, the members remained active until their capture in June 1972 along with other leading members of the RAF. Their trial lasted for four years. In May 1976, Meinhof hung herself in Stammheim Prison, Stuttgart; it is probable that she had become distressed by the direction being taken by the RAF's terrorism. Their trials finally over and found guilty and all hope of release or rescue ended, Baader, Ensslin, Mahler and Jan-Carl Raspe committed suicide in their Stammheim cells on 18 October 1977. The next day, the RAF hostage Hanns Martin Schleyer was found dead in the boot of a car.

In broad terms the ideology of the Red Army Faction was similar to that of the Socialist German Students' Association – a socialist society for Germany and a strong emphasis on developing world liberation movements. The Red Army Faction, however, combined the SDS ideology with a justification for armed action: in essence, propaganda by the deed. In the summer of 1970,

The Red Army Faction, however, combined the SDS ideology with a justification for armed action: in essence, propaganda by the deed

the RAF made contact with the Palestine terrorist groups. At first the RAF's attacks were directed at property and they engaged in bank robberies, but their actions moved on to killing people. The first victim was a policeman; they dehumanized their victims as 'pigs': 'We say that policemen are pigs, that guy in uniform is a pig; he is not a human being. *And we behave toward him accordingly*' wrote Ulrike Meinhof (della Porta 1995, 173). The use of 'pig' was doubly insensitive in Germany with its anti-Semitic, Nazi history. In May 1972, the RAF justified an attack in Heidelberg, on the American headquarters in Europe, in terms of the Vietnam War being a genocide similar to the 'final solution' and Auschwitz.

The attack in Heidelberg began a series of bombings in which indiscriminate killing featured, including one at the Springer building in Hamburg, which killed 17 people. Baader, Meinhof and Ensslin were captured along with 18 other members of the RAF in June 1972. Their hunger strikes and protests in prison were used as further justification for RAF action. Related groups, most notably the June Second Movement (*Bewegung 2. Juni*, which took its name from the date of Benno Ohnesorg's death), also carried on the terrorism. In this second wave of terrorism the connection with the Middle East became closer. The West German parliament introduced yet stronger anti-terrorist legislation.

The trials of the RAF members captured back in 1972 finally came to an end in July 1977. The new wave of terrorism reached a climax in September of that year with the German RAF and Palestinian PFLP (Popular Front for the Liberation of Palestine) hijacking a Lufthansa airliner in Majorca. Of this incident of international terrorism more will be learnt in Chapter 8. Its failure led, directly, to the leading RAF members committing suicide in their cells.

The Red Brigades

Italy had a history of authoritarianism in ways similar to Germany's but, with its fascist rather than Nazi past, lacked the guilt of the Holocaust. In Germany at the end of the war the Nazi Party had been demolished and legislation introduced to ban extremist parties; in Italy, although Mussolini's Fascist Party, *Partido Nationale Fascista* (PNF), was banned a legal neo-fascist party, the *Movimento Sociale Italiana* (MSI), was established in 1946. Furthermore, Italy also retained a strong Communist Party (PCI, *Partito Comunista Italiano*). With both communist and fascist parties, the cleavage between Catholics and communists/ socialists remained strong.

In the 1950s and 1960s workers' strikes and demonstrations produced a harsh reaction by the Christian Democrat ruling party, which viewed the strikes not simply as protests for higher wages and better working conditions but as opposition to the political system as a whole. During that time hundreds of strikers and demonstrators were killed by the police. As in Germany, the Christian Democrats dominated in the post-war coalitions and there was another parallel in the participation of the Italian Socialist Party (PSI, *Partito Socialista Italiano*) in the centre-left coalition in the early 1960s that failed to produce the reforms promised. Perceptions of the potential for radical change through legitimate political opposition were thereby undermined and the young Italian New Leftists, like their German counter-parts, rejected the system as undemocratic and came to view violence as their only option against an authoritarian system. There was, however, also an important difference: in Italy, New Left protest met not only with a government that viewed a violent response as the only appropriate reaction to the protest but also with counter-action from neo-fascists.

In Italy, the outbreak of right-wing terrorism preceded the outbreak of left-wing terrorism

In Italy, the outbreak of right-wing terrorism preceded the outbreak of left-wing terrorism. Neo-fascist violence began with the intimidation of the New Left protesters, escalated and then moved on to what became known as the 'strategy of tension', a name coined by the British newspaper *The Observer*. The strategy involved an anonymous bombing campaign directed at the public. Both the violence and the bombings grew more intense following the development of a workers' movement proclaiming itself 'anti-authoritarian' that erupted alongside the students' movement.

The right-wing terror campaign was at its height from 1969 to 1974, during which time bombings of trains and areas where processions and demonstrations by the left were designated escalated and attacks on militants, including assassinations, mounted. In Rome alone more than 700 violent acts took place, although, through the loose organization of the terrorism, many of the acts have never been attributed to a specific organization. The most dramatic examples of right-wing bombings occurred in December 1969 when 16 innocent people were killed and

90 more were injured in Piazza Fontana, Milan, and in 1974, when 12 people died and 48 were injured on a train travelling between Florence and Bologna.

The trial, held in 1974, for the December 1969 bombing in Milan exposed the government, the police and the secret services in their responsibility for having misdirected the investigations into the bombings away from the right towards the left. The state's actions set the conditions for the spate of neo-fascist bombings through to 1974 and, indeed, on to the Bologna Central Station bombing in 1980, in which 84 people were killed and a further 150 injured. This, coupled with the state's failure to solve any of these extreme-right bombings and to successfully prosecute the perpetrators, has ensured that the suspicion of state involvement, endorsement and even commissions has persisted.

Although the Red Brigades (*Brigate Rosse*) were founded in 1970 with the express purpose of fighting the neo-fascists, the Red Brigades killed no one until 1974. Their first victims were two young neo-fascists. Before these killings the Red Brigades engaged in kidnappings. From 1974 to 1976, kidnappings and assassinations, primarily of executives, journalists, police officers and magistrates, then escalated, culminating, in 1978, in the most famous example of the kidnap and murder of Aldo Moro, the leader of the Christian Democrats. From that point, the violence increased and the targeting of victims became more arbitrary, for example employees (executives and foremen) of the car manufacturers Fiat and Alfa Romeo, and a factory worker, Guido Rossa, who was both a union delegate and a member of the Italian Communist Party.

Teasing out general lessons on the formation and organization of terrorist groups

Both grievances about lack of representation of interests and its consequences and experience of the escalation of violence following heavy-handed government responses to protest action were clearly common factors in the development of the RAF, the Red Brigades, the IRA/PIRA and ETA. But, there were also clear differences between the four cases. The PIRA in Northern Ireland and ETA-M in Spain were sections that broke away from existing clandestine groups, the IRA and ETA, both of which had wider nationalist support groups, outgrowths of Irish and Basque histories, respectively. The RAF in Germany and the Red Brigades in Italy broke not from existing clandestine groups but from mass movements openly engaged in protest; and these movements were left-wing not nationalist.

Explanations for the RAF and Red Brigades emphasize the differences between the new social movements of the New Left as compared with the class movements of the 'old left'

Explanations for the RAF and Red Brigades emphasize the differences between the new social movements of the New Left as compared with the class movements of the 'old left'. The new social movements of late-capitalism (such as students' movements) lack political organizations such as trade unions and workers' political parties and their goals, unlike demands about economic production, are not negotiable through the political system. Their ambition is to change social values. Lacking identity with class communities, complex political ideas, such as those of Marxism-Leninism, are reduced to simplification and distorted into vulgar doctrines (Melucci, 1981).

A 'cycle of protest' (della Porta and Tarrow, 1986) is also involved. In this cycle, violent tactics are adopted as a strategy to compensate for decline in mass protest. Semi-clandestine groups, which go on to choose terrorism as their major tactic, appear at the point where mass support is at its lowest ebb. People get tired of being mobilized towards the same goal; members of radical left groups who set out with the hope of changing the world eventually return home or go back to complete their academic studies. As support dwindles, competition takes place between groups for support from a dwindling set of radicals and it is this that leads to a rise in violence. As this violence grows so the demands being made become less precise and some of these groups that have adopted dramatic forms of violence, by then only a tiny proportion of the original New Left supporters, then take that final step into becoming organized terrorist groups. The cycle of protest in respect of the civil rights marches may also have played a part in the splitting off of the PIRA and the development of democracy, post-Franco, similarly may have affected the development of ETA-M.

Once the decision has been made to go underground, mostly prompted by the need to hide having committed an illegal violent act (Baader and Ensslin provide an excellent example of this) the isolation brings a distance from reality and a desensitization to the effects of terrorist actions on innocent victims. This distance from reality is nicely illustrated by the comment made by Marie MacGuire, a member of PIRA, when describing a car bomb in Belfast in 1972, which killed 6 and injured 146:

I admit that at times I did not connect with the people who were killed or injured in such explosions. I always judged such deaths in terms of the effect they would have on our support, and felt that this in turn depended upon how many people accepted our 'explanation'.

(Marie MacGuire, quoted in Crenshaw, 1992)

'Our "explanation"', PIRA's explanation that is, involved blaming the security forces for deliberately muddling the telephone warning. By sending coded warnings to the police beforehand the claim made by the PIRA was that the deaths of innocents killed by the bomb explosions were not the fault of those who planted the bombs but the fault of the police who failed to act effectively, clearing the area in time. As Marie MacGuire further explains: 'the movement accepted responsibility for the explosion and it was a curious thing that the Provisionals felt that by doing so they somehow atoned for the casualties.' By distancing themselves, in their rationalization, it was not the innocents but themselves, the terrorists, who were the victims.

Organization

As the examples of the PIRA and ETA as compared with the RAF and the Red Brigades have shown, terrorist organizations differ in respect of the extent to which they rely on wider support in society and also in their size. Large organizations, such as the IRA and ETA, are cellular with a hierarchical, ladder-like command structure. In this structure only those at the top know who the leadership is. The organization of small groups, such as the Red Army Faction, the Italian Red Brigades, which, like *Narodnaya Volya* (The People's Will) in Russia in the late nineteenth century, do not depend on wider support, resemble more the structure of a wheel. In the wheel-like structure the leader rather than being at the top of a hierarchy is at the centre of the organization, in direct contact with each member of the group.

Organizational theory suggests that these designs, the 'cellular' (or 'ladder-like') and the 'wheel-like' (also termed the 'centrifugal' system) (Zawodny, 1981; Crenshaw, 1985) are chosen both to best protect the terrorist organization and to ensure its continuation, ready for action. These designs help to minimize the spread of discontent while, at the same time, maximizing calculations against exit. In protecting secrecy within the organization, they also minimize the damage that a terrorist who manages to exit successfully from the terrorist group may do when passing on information about the members and workings of the organization.

The goal of the survival is also reflected in innovations in the strategies and tactics employed by the terrorist groups: the aim is to stay at least one step ahead of the authorities. The current vogue adopted by other groups for that oddly distasteful phenomenon of the suicide-

> *The goal of the survival is also reflected in innovations in the strategies and tactics employed by the terrorist groups: the aim is to stay at least one step ahead of the authorities*

bomber, the guilty blown up along with innocent victims, is the perfect antidote to the perpetrator, once captured, turning informer.

Recommended reading

For very informative chapters on each of the four principal cases, see Martha Crenshaw, ed., *Terrorism in Context* (University Park, PAI: Pennsylvanian State University Press, 1995) and especially Peter Merkl, 'West German Left-Wing Terrorism', G. Shabad and F.J. Llera Ramo, 'Political Violence in a Democratic State: Basque Terrorism in Spain', and Donatella della Porta, 'Left-Wing Terrorism in Italy'. For an excellent comparative study of the RAF and the Red Brigades, see Donatella della Porta, *Social Movements, Political Violence, and the State: A Comparative Analysis of Italy and Germany* (Cambridge: Cambridge University Press, 1995).

For full-length individual studies, the following are recommended: The IRA/PIRA: Richard English *Armed Struggle: The History of the IRA* (London: Pan Books, 2004); John McGarry and Brendan O'Leary, *Explaining Northern Ireland: Broken Images* (Oxford: Blackwell, 1995). ETA: John Sullivan, *ETA and Basque Nationalism: The Fight for Euskadi, 1890–1986* (London: Routledge, 1988). The RAF: Stefan Aust, *The Baader–Meinhof Group* (London: Bodley Head, 1987). The Red Brigades: Robert C. Meade, Jr, *The Red Brigades: The Story of Italian Terrorism* (New York: St Martin's Press, 1990). For terrorism in Europe in general, see Jan Oskar Engene, *Terrorism in Europe: Explaining the Trends Since 1950* (Cheltenham: Edward Elgar, 2004).

CHAPTER 7

Terrorist groups and repressive regimes

THE NOTION OF A STRATEGY FOR state overthrow based on the 'propaganda by the deed' would be absurd under a terror regime: spontaneous thinking is stopped, control of the media is total and the terror system would ensure that no terrorist group would have a chance of survival. Like terror regimes, repressive dictatorships, too, seek to destroy opposition and to deny access to information. With enough repression they may be successful in defeating terrorist groups: Marighela quickly found this to his cost in Brazil. Although ironic, this is why the most enduring and most notorious terrorist groups have developed not under the most repressive regimes but where democratic structures are present, for it is the more open societies that provide opportunities for terrorist groups. The presence of terrorist groups has also led governments intent on democracy to turn to violent repression. A striking example is Sendero Luminoso (the Shining Path), in Peru.

Sendero Luminoso (the Shining Path)

Sendero Luminoso first made its appearance as a terrorist group in May 1980. It did so at a time not of heightening government repression but the opposite. In May 1980 the first elections were being held in Peru since the military took power in 1968, the last presidential election having taken place in 1963: Marxist parties were among those standing in the 1980 election.

The Shining Path

Sendero Luminoso began in 1962 as the Huamanga command of the *Ejército de Liberación* (ELN, National Liberation Army), a rural guerrilla movement, which was at the National University of San Cristóbal de Huamanga in Ayacucho, a rural department in the south-central Peruvian highlands. From 1963, the leader of the Huamanga command was Abimael Guzmán Reynoso, a young philosophy lecturer. The Huamanga command broke away in 1965; rejecting foco theory, they adopted a more Maoist position on rural strategy in which a Communist Party guerrilla army is crucial. By 1966 they were part of the Communist Party of Peru – Red Flag (*Pertido Communista del Peru – Bandera Roja*, PCP-BR) but they were expelled some time between 1968 and 1970.

In 1970 the Guzmán group took the title of *Pertido Communista del Peru en el Sendero Luminoso de Mariátegui*, shortened by outsiders to Sendero Luminoso. Mariátegui was a Peruvian intellectual and founder, in 1928, of the original Communist Party of Peru. He theorized on primitive communism in its pure Indian version. Nearly 90 per cent of Ayacucho's population was composed of Quechua-speaking Indians and the area, rather enclosed and inaccessible, was one of the poorest in Peru. The years to 1978 were spent developing relationships with local peasant communities and studying and eventually synthesizing the ideas of Mao and Mariátegui. In 1978, the year in which, in elections, they lost their dominant position in the university to a more moderate group and the military government of Peru began the return to civilian government with an election for a constituent assembly, Sendero Luminoso went underground.

Between 1980 and the end of 1992 Sendero Luminoso carried out an estimated 23,610 killings and at least 3,000 disappearances. Guzmán was captured in September 1992.

Sendero Luminoso's first acts in the 1980 elections were the burning of ballot boxes in one of the local peasant communities with which they had interacted in the 1970s. They also hung dead dogs from lampposts in Lima, the capital, with signs saying 'Deng Xiaoping, Son of a Bitch' (Degregori, 1992). Bombing of buildings moved on to assassinations of public figures, escalating to more indiscriminate violence and then the violence expanded; the start to this expansion was signalled by a jailbreak of Senderistas from the main Ayacucho prison in 1982. In August of that year electricity supplies were bombed. In the blackout, teams of terrorists drove through the streets of Lima throwing sticks of dynamite into shops, banks and public buildings. A similar blackout occurred at the end of the year and then began bombings of cinemas, restaurants, anywhere that people gathered. Tourist hotels and foreign-owned businesses and embassies and the like – even a beauty contest – then began to be attacked (McCormick, 2001).

The first state of emergency was declared in 1981 and in December 1982 a 'Military Emergency Zone' was declared, with the army taking administrative control in seven provinces in and around Ayacucho. By 1983, Senderista terrorist cells were in more than half of Peru's provinces; further areas were taken under army control in 1985. Abuses by the military became rife

> *Abuses by the military became rife but Sendero's early base of support had soon been lost by their terrorist behaviour. Any peasants resisting their authority were dealt with brutally: killing, maiming, indiscriminate destruction of crops and livestock, and so on*

but Sendero's early base of support had soon been lost by their terrorist behaviour. Any peasants resisting their authority were dealt with brutally: killing, maiming, indiscriminate destruction of crops and livestock, and so on.

In 1985 another presidential election took place, accompanied by Sendero car bombings, jail riots and assassinations; an opposition candidate was elected. In 1986, Sendero stepped up the bombing of restaurants, shopping areas and banks. In reaction, the Peruvian armed forces engaged in massacres. By the early 1990s Sendero Luminoso actions had spread to most regions of Peru and the Cultivireni mission, the communal quarters of the Asháninkas, had become a major target. The Asháninkas are one of the largest Indian groups in the Peruvian Amazon and they resisted demands for recruits to Sendero. In 1989, armed with sub-machine guns and assault rifles Senderistas not only attacked and burned the mission but also crucified the head teacher. In February 1990 they killed 15 more of the unarmed Indians and went on to massacre in other villages: a further 55 were killed, others were mutilated, including 14 children, their ears being sliced off (Palmer, 1995). The run-up to the 1990 election again faced car bombings, sabotage and assassinations. By 1991 there were somewhere between 3,000 and 5,000 Senderistas. In 1992 Alberto Fujimori, the new president, went all out to defeat Sendero; this was how Guzmán was captured. From his cell in 1993 he pronounced that the Senderistas should give up the armed struggle but car bombings in Lima showed that not all had been persuaded.

This escalation of violence, on both sides, and the growth into a large insurgent force are also characteristic of the most enduring of all developing world terrorist groups: the Tamil Tigers. They, however, are based neither on a version of Maoist ideology nor on a communist party.

The Tamil Tigers (LTTE)

The Liberation Tigers of Tamil Eelam (LTTE) developed in Sri Lanka (Ceylon before it was granted independence from Britain in 1948), which had at the time one of the most democratic political systems in the developing world. It was one of only a handful of countries where alteration of government took place through elections, that is to say where an opposition party formed the new government. In 1972, however, Sirimavo Bandarnaike, prime minister of the Sri Lankan Freedom Party (SLFP) government, elected in 1970, amended the constitution so as to disadvantage the three million Tamils who constituted 17 per cent of the population. The amendment to the constitution made Sinhala the official language, so ruling out Tamil, and also privileged Buddhism as the pre-eminent religion. Tamils were either Hindu or Christian. In response the main Tamil political parties, the Federal Party, representing the Tamils of the northern region of Jaffna, and the Ceylon Workers' Party, the party of the Indian Tamils of the central parts of Sri Lanka, created the Tamil United Front (TUF), but stayed committed to the parliamentary process.

Mrs Bandarnaike had enforced measures that were anti-Tamil, when prime minister in an earlier government, from 1960 to 1965. She lost the election in 1965. In the late 1960s an informal militant alternative to the Federal Party, the Tamil Eelam Liberation Organization (TELO), was started (*Eelam* means 'homeland'). In 1970 Sivakumaran, a member of the Tamil Student's League (TSL), attempted to assassinate a government minister. In the following year, he tried to assassinate the mayor of Jaffna, a Tamil. Trapped by police when later carrying out a bank robbery, he committed suicide by swallowing a cyanide pill. A potassium cyanide capsule, hung round the neck, was eventually to be carried by every Tamil Tiger. In 1975, another attempt to assassinate the mayor of Jaffna was made, this time successfully; he was shot by a 17-year-old, Velupillai Pirabhakaran. With the 500,000 rupees that he acquired through a bank raid, in 1976, Pirabhakaran then founded the Tamil New Tigers, later renamed the Liberation Tigers of Tamil Eelan (LTTE).

In 1978 the LTTE tried out something new, an act that clearly identified them as a terrorist group: they exploded a time bomb on an Air Ceylon passenger jet

In 1978 the LTTE tried out something new, an act that clearly identified them as a terrorist group: they exploded a time bomb on an Air Ceylon passenger jet. The Tamil Tigers were also to become the first group to engage in suicide bombing and also then to carry out such bombings abroad. Most famously, in May 1991, a young woman Tamil Tiger, Dhanu, acted as a 'human bomb', killing the former prime minister of India, Rajiv Gandhi, as he held a general election meeting in a town near Madras, India. In the explosion 17 others were also killed. The LTTE then assassinated Ranasinghe Premadasa, the president of Sri Lanka, in 1993. In January 1996 a suicide bomber crashed a lorry loaded with high explosives and shrapnel into the Central Bank in the commercial sector of Sri Lanka's capital, Colombo. In the explosion nearly 100 people were killed and over 1,600 were injured.

From a group of 40 or so Tamil Tigers in the early 1980s, by the mid-1980s they numbered around 3,000 and by the mid-1990s had reached an estimated total of 16,000. By this point the LTTE produced their combat uniforms and, beginning in 1991, engaged in conventional warfare: pitched battles. By the 1990s the LTTE was also producing its own mines, mortars, grenades and explosive devices; they even had mini-submarines and suicide bombers were training to fly small aircraft that have the advantage of being undetectable on radar screens (Joshi, 1996).

The growth of the LTTE into an army followed the ambush and killing of 13 soldiers in July 1983: it led to riots breaking out, with the Sinhalese attacking Tamils and killing Tamil militant leaders held in jail. Two consequences were crucial. First, hundreds of thousands of Tamils moved to the north-eastern provinces while nearly all the Sinhalese left the north and moved south. This established a geographical distinction between the Tamils and Sinhalese and so reinforced the claim for *Eelam*. Second, streams of Tamils left Sri Lanka to become refugees in Tamil Nadu, the Indian state in which 60 million Tamils live, across the narrow stretch of water, the Palk Strait. This generated financial support from abroad, and not only in India; it also brought practical support in the form of training by India's external intelligence agency, the Research and Analysis Wing.

The events of 1983 turned into a civil war, broken only by the years when the Indian army acted as a peacekeeping force between July 1987 and March 1990, during which time the LTTE fought the Indian troops. The terrain of north-eastern Sri Lanka ensured that the LTTE was able to combine guerrilla warfare with terrorism. Adding to the conflict, the Janantha Vimukthi Peramu (People's Liberation Front), an anti-India, nationalist Sinhala group with strong support in the south, declared war on the government for its collaboration with the 'India invader'. In the violence that ensued around 40,000 people were killed by state-sponsored death squads. Three months after the Indian troops left in March 1990, the Tigers declared war on the Colombo government.

Tentative lessons on underlying conditions

Heavy-handed government policies, insensitive to minority ethnic interests, that sought to educate and promote the language and religion of the majority clearly played a major part in leading to the violence out of which a terrorist group became established in Sri Lanka. The situation had then been compounded by geographical movement, which established regional separation. Under colonialism, the Tamil minority had been educated and privileged over the Sinhalese majority. Similar historical lessons about the effects of colonialism and conflicts of group interests involving religious, ethnic and language differences later reinforced by movements of people and regional separation are also to be found in the Punjab, India. There, as in Sri Lanka, terrorist group action developed in reaction against the electoral process, even though in India government policies are strikingly more sensitive to minority needs.

Khalistani Sikh groups

Under British colonialism Sikhs constituted approximately 14 per cent of the population of the Punjab, with Muslims at around 52 per cent and Hindus around 30 per cent. At the end of colonialism, in 1947, under partition, the larger Muslim-majority part of the state of Punjab became part of the newly formed country of Pakistan. With Hindus and Sikhs also moving in order to remain in India, in the new Punjab Hindus formed the new majority: Hindus nearly two-thirds of the population and Sikhs at one-third. Although the common theme of Sikh protests is that the Sikh 'panth' (religion) is under threat, while violence was usual in past movements, under colonialism non-violent Sikh political movements became the norm, with the Akali Dal party emerging as the largest Sikh party. After partition the Akali Dal successfully campaigned for Sikh equality with Hindus and for recognition for both official and educational purposes of the Punjabi language and the Gurmukhi script. The party also campaigned for the Punjab to be divided in terms of the dominant use of language and eventually for a separate Sikh state: Punjabi Suba.

In 1960 hostilities led to tens of thousands of arrests but though militant the Punjabi Suba movement used non-violent tactics. In 1966 a limited version of a separate Sikh state was achieved, reduced, in essence, to the central plains, Sikhs became the majority 60 per cent of the population of a new state,

Haryana, created out of south-east Punjab; northern regions of the Punjab became part of an enlarged Himachal Pradesh. In the elections of 1967, however, not the Akali Dal but the Congress Party won the largest number of seats. The Akali Dal (Sikh) and the Jan Sangh (Hindu) parties allied to form an anti-Congress United Front and won two later elections but, in 1979, the second alliance government led to a split among Akalis. In the 1980 elections the Congress Party won a decisive majority in Punjab.

Sikh terrorism began in the Punjab in September 1981. Its sources, the first back in 1978, were the speeches made by Sant Jarnail Singh Bhindranwale. In these speeches he combined a political message – that Sikhs must not be ruled over by Hindus – with the glorification of violence as the means not simply for achieving independence but for preserving both the true Sikh religion and the true Sikh community – Khalistan. Khalistan is a utopian goal; though ideally intended as a Sikh-controlled state independent from India, its geographical boundaries are vague and, in practice, it may or may not incorporate Sikhs as the majority.

Sant Jarnail Singh Bhindranwale

Sant Jarnail Singh Bhindranwale was the head of a religious seminary. In his speeches he argued the justification for violence and terrorism as the means for achieving the pure Sikh religion and the true Sikh community, Khalistan. By 1984, Bhindranwale was ensconsed in the Golden Temple complex at Amritsar, issuing Guru-like commands and judgements.

Violence is not an inherent part of the Sikh religion and in glorifying violence Bhindranwale privileged the ideas and practices of the tenth prophet, Guru Gobind Singh, over those of other prophets and, not least, those of the founder of the

Sikh faith, Guru Nanak (1469–1538). Gobind Singh was a warrior-leader; Guru Nanak was a pious man who sought to smooth out differences between sects through appeasement. The Sikh religion was a development from the Hindu religion. From 1526, the Punjab was part of the Mughal empire, with Muslims the majority, and this remained so under British colonialism, which began in 1849.

> *Violence is not an inherent part of the Sikh religion and in glorifying violence Bhindranwale privileged the ideas and practices of the tenth prophet, Guru Gobind Singh, over those of other prophets*

In 1699, Guru Gobind Singh, the warrior-leader, called Sikhs together to fight for the new *khalsa*, the pure Sikh society, and introduced rules that made male Sikhs clearly distinguishable from both Muslims and Hindus. Most strikingly, they were forbidden to cut their hair and each was required to carry a sword. He also resolved the problem of the Guru's succession by permanently transferring the guruship, on his death, from residing in a person to residence in the community of Sikhs and in the holy book, the *Guru Granth Sahib*.

Bhindranwale cast himself as the present-day Guru Gobind Singh. Conjuring the image of the small minority against the vast majority, assassination was chosen as the means of Bhindranwale's movement and the reward for martyrdom, the giving of his or her life for the *khalsa*, was proclaimed eternal.

In response to the violence and terrorism, in 1983 the Indian government introduced president's rule in the Punjab. During May 1984, there were more than 50 incidents a week, including arson, bank robberies and attacks on police, but also indiscriminate bombings and shootings and the killing of passengers

forced off buses. In June, the Indian government stopped negotiations over state autonomy and, using around 70,000 Indian
army troops, undertook military occupation of the state of
Punjab including conducting a huge military operation against the
Golden Temple complex. In two days an estimated 1,000 people
were killed in fighting around the Golden Temple, around 400
of them pilgrims. Bhindranwale, along with other Sikh leaders,
was killed.

Violence and terrorism continued and, on 31 October 1984,
Prime Minister Indira Gandhi was assassinated by two of her
bodyguards, both Sikhs. In places throughout India, violence in
retaliation for the assassination was immediate: near to 3,000
Sikhs were killed, their properties were set on fire and Sikh
temples were attacked, hundreds of them in India's capital,
Delhi. Furthermore, police cooperation was involved in these
events and charges were made that the Congress Party, Indira
Gandhi's party, was complicit. Around 50,000 Sikhs from all
over India fled to the Punjab.

Following the Congress Party's victory in the national
elections in December 1984, which installed Rajiv Gandhi,
Indira Ghandi's son, as prime minister, a period of reconciliation opened. Though marked by the Punjab Accord of July 1985
the opening of reconciliation had little effect. Terrorism continued, with a new tactic of bombs inside transistor radios left
mostly at bus and railway stations. Nineteen such bombs
exploded in Delhi on 10–11 May 1985, with neighbouring Indian
states also affected. The following month, on 23 June, a new
tactic was employed by Sikh terrorists: 329 passengers and
crew were killed when an Air India aeroplane was blown up in
flight over the Irish Sea. The same day a bomb was planted on an

Air India plane at Narita airport, Tokyo; it killed two baggage handlers.

After just under two years, Punjab returned to president's rule. In July 1987 seven Sikhs brandishing guns forced Hindu passengers off a bus in Punjab and then shot and killed 32 of them and wounded a further 38. The following night Sikh terrorists boarded another two buses near the Punjab border and killed a total of 36 passengers. Under Section 5 of the Terrorist and Disruptive Activities (Prevention) Act of 1987, the whole of the state of Punjab became a 'notified area'. In February 1988 the *Times of India* reported that at least 254 people had been killed by terrorists, including assassinations of politicians and police, just since the start of the year (Wallace, 1995). The newspaper also reported in that year that a total of 167 terrorist groups were involved, all but 22 of them part of the network of one of four major groups: Babbar Khalsan, the most zealously religious; the Bindranwale Tiger Force (BTF); the Khalistan Liberation Force (KLF); and the Khalistan Commando Force (KCF).

In March 1988, under the Fifty-ninth Constitutional Amendment, a state of emergency was declared in Punjab. Two months later another military operation took place in the Golden Temple complex. This time the operation, led by the Black Cat Commandos of the National Security Guards and including 3,000 paramilitary soldiers, was restrained; controlled and under media scrutiny, with live coverage, there was little loss of life. At least 156 terrorists surrendered. The killing, however, did not stop.

Factional fighting between Sikh groups combined with the use of modern weapons such as assault rifles, anti-tank rockets, rocket-launchers and bombs, including plastic explosives and mines, led to an increase in the number of deaths, especially in 1990 and 1991. By 1992, there were around 4,000 active terrorists. Extortion and smuggling helped to finance operations. The escalation of violence was also the consequence of heavy-handed state reaction to the terrorist group action. Large numbers of government paramilitary groups were ranged against the Khalistani groups, some 70,000 police and paramilitary in 1988 and many new battalions raided in the years following. The Punjab remained under president's rule until 1992 when law and order began to return and turnout in elections rose dramatically. By the end of 1993, in addition to the deaths of thousands of terrorists and policeman more than 10,000 civilians had lost their lives.

Similar historical lessons to those of Sri Lanka and India about conflicts of group interests involving religious, ethnic and language differences, which are then compounded by movements of people, by regional separation and claims over land, are also conditions found in the Middle East.

The Middle East

As in India, in the Middle East, the effects of empire and mixing of peoples with different religions, languages and ethnicity began before colonialism. The Ottoman Empire, which at its peak ruled over north Africa, the Middle East, south-east Europe and Anatolia (Turkey), in 1914 covered parts of the Middle East and Anatolia. In the First World War the Ottoman Empire sided with Germany and after their defeat in 1918 the Middle East was divided between Britain and France for rule through a mandate, granted by the League of Nations. France took control of Syria and Lebanon; Britain took control of Trans-Jordan (today's Jordan), Mesopotamia (today's Iraq) and Palestine. The mandated territories were intended eventually to become independent but for the interim they were to be ruled in much the same way as if colonies.

Palestine under British mandate covered, approximately, modern Israel including both the West Bank and the Gaza Strip. In 1922, the population of 752,000 people contained 650,000 Arabs (most of them Muslims, with around 10 per cent Christian Arabs) and 84,000 Jews. The size of the Jewish population then grew through immigration, which greatly increased once Hitler and the Nazi Party ruled Germany, from 1933. In 1931 the number of Jews entering Palestine was just over 4,000; ten times that number entered in 1934; the number entering in 1935 was nearly 62,000. Unlike the original Palestinian Jews, the new settlers neither spoke nor understood Arabic.

In protest against Jewish immigration and their purchasing of land in Palestine the Arabs organized a general strike in April 1936 and argued for a majority Arab government to be established. Riots soon erupted, as they had in 1929, and before long spontaneous armed Arab

In protest against Jewish immigration and their purchasing of land in Palestine the Arabs organized a general strike in April 1936 and argued for a majority Arab government to be established

rebellion had broken out spreading across the whole of Palestine directed against both the British mandate authorities and the Jewish settlers. The rebellion lasted until 1939; during the rebellion atrocities occurred and out of these atrocities terrorist groups took form. The main Palestinian Arab terrorist group was al-Futuwwah, which was under the leadership of the grand mufti of Jerusalem, but it was the Jewish groups that became famous.

In 1931, a breakaway group of Haganah, the Jewish defence force founded in 1921, illegally formed a paramilitary attacking force: the Irgun Zvai Leumi. Like the Arabs, the Irgun wanted Britain to leave Palestine but their view of the future independent state, as a Jewish state, was quite different from that of the Arabs. In July 1938, the British executed a Jewish youth for shooting at Arabs on a bus. In retaliation Irgun exploded land mines in the Arab fruit market at Haifa. In the worst single act of terrorism in Palestine, up to that point, 74 innocent victims were killed and a further 129 were wounded. Further attacks were mostly on British facilities and properties but with the outbreak of the Second World War and Britain's stand against Hitler, Zionists, that is Jewish supporters of a Jewish state of Israel, actively supported Britain. There was, however, an exception: the Stern Gang.

In 1940, an extreme underground terrorist group broke away from Irgun – Lehi, or the 'Stern Gang' after its leader Avraham Stern – to continue the fight against Britain. In its contorted logic the Stern Gang sided with Germany and furthered its notoriety by assassinating Lord Moyne, the British minister-resident in the Middle East, in Cairo, in 1944. After this assassination Haganah helped the British to round up Stern terrorists and also Irgun terrorists for deportation. Following the defeat of Hitler in 1945, attacks on the British in Israel resumed. In July 1946, Irgun blew up the King David Hotel in Jerusalem, which lodged British troops and was also the British administration's social centre. Dressed as Arabs, Irgun terrorists placed bombs in the basement of the hotel and telephoned warnings, which were not passed on correctly. The bombs killed 91 and wounded 45 people: some were British soldiers, others were indiscriminately killed Arabs and Jews.

In August 1947 a Special Committee on Palestine, appointed by the United Nations, recommended that Palestine be partitioned into an Arab state and a Jewish state. This was agreed by the UN in November 1947, along with the decision that the

In August 1947 a Special Committee on Palestine, appointed by the United Nations, recommended that Palestine be partitioned into an Arab state and a Jewish state

British mandate would be ended in 1948. Fighting immediately broke out between Arabs and Jews. In May 1948, when the state of Israel became a reality at the end of the British mandate, the civil war became the first Arab–Israeli war. The Arab forces were soon supported by troops from Egypt, Syria, Iraq and Lebanon.

At the end of the First Arab–Israeli War, in 1949, Israel's allotted land allocation under the 1947 United Nations partition plan of 57 per cent of Palestine became 77 per cent. With the Arabs defeated and thus no Palestinian state the territory that remained came under the control of Arab countries: the West Bank under the rule of Trans-Jordan, the Gaza-Rafiah area under the control of Egypt. The lack of coherent Arab policy for Palestine, which had contributed to the Arab defeat, ensured that inter-Arab conflict would continue. The mass emigration of Arabs from the state of Israel to the surrounding Arab countries also ensured that fighting against Israel would continue;

Palestinian resistance fighters, fedayeen, developed among the refugees. The mass emigration also ensured not simply that terrorism would continue but that it would take on an international aspect.

In 1951, a Palestinian terrorist assassinated King Abdullah of Trans-Jordan in Jerusalem, where he was involved in peace talks with Israel. From 1954, following Gamal Abdel Nasser's becoming prime minister of Egypt, fedayeen raids from the Gaza Strip and from Jordan were sponsored by Egypt. In 1955, a fedayeen commando unit was established in the Gaza under the Egyptian army. Only some of these were Palestinians but out of them Yasser Arafat formed al-Fatah, a group that, in view of its eventual adoption of international terrorism, will be covered in the next chapter. The ideas behind al-Fatah, initially at least, were Islamic values in line with those of the Muslim Brotherhood, which had been set up in Egypt in 1928. Importantly, the guerrilla strategy adopted by al-Fatah drew on the example of the Algerian FLN, a case noted in Chapter 2 for having adopted terrorist tactics. Algeria also shared similarities with Palestine under mandate.

The Algerian FLN

The Front de Libération Nationale (FLN) formed in Algeria in 1954 as a nationalist organization aiming for separation from France through armed struggle. Strictly, Algeria was an administrative region of France, not its colony, but force, not equal citizenship, was the basis of French rule. The majority of Algerians were Muslim Arabs. Almost a million of the total ten million population of Algeria in 1954, however, were settlers of

European origin and not therefore Muslims, around half of them descendants of the French who had settled there in the nineteenth century and the other half being of various Mediterranean origins. Riots occurred in Sétif in 1945. They left nearly 100 Europeans dead and were brutally put down by the French authorities: villages were bombed and summary executions carried out. Added to this, settlers formed vigilante groups. The number of Algerians killed after the Muslim riots was at least 6,000–8,000 (Crenshaw Hutchinson, 1978).

After the Sétif riots the *Movement pour le Triomphe des Libertés Democratiques*, a nationalist organization, was formed, which set up the *Organisation Spéciale* (OS) in 1950, on which the FLN was based. When, in 1956, they took the decision to adopt terrorism, Larbi Ben M'Hidé argued for the importance of not simply military combat but acts that could, at one and the same time, seize the imagination of the Algerian masses and undermine the French colonial authority's conviction in their right and ability to rule. His argument was much in line with the idea of 'propaganda by the deed': the expectation was that the dramatic act would lead to a mass uprising. The urban terrorism opened by the FLN's underground force, the *Zone Autonome d'Alger* (ZAA), at the start of the Battle of Algiers in 1956 produced the expected state terrorism reaction but it did not lead to the theorized mass insurrection.

Following the defeat of the ZAA, a counter-intelligence operation was launched through which local leaders of rural *wilayas*, the political-juridical districts, were convinced that those fleeing the cities were 'traitors'. Those in flight from the French forces were met in the rural areas, therefore, not with support but with torture. An estimated 2,000 Algerians died as a consequence. In

August 1958, the FLN adopted the new strategy of attacking targets in France, including police stations, munitions factories and oil refineries. This new terrorist campaign was brought to a halt by the FLN's provisional Algerian government, GPRA; it formed in 1958 after President de Gaulle's election, though he refused to recognize it as the legitimate sole representative of Algerians.

FLN terrorism then moved back to Algeria, at first bombing department stores and then carrying out bus explosions. Again, however, the theory was thwarted by practice. In opposition to the FLN, a right-wing terrorist group – the *Organisation d'Armée Secrète* (OAS) – was set up, in 1960, to fight against Algerian independence. The OAS was modelled on the FLN or, at least, on their interpretation of its organization, in particular the underground cellular structure in Algiers, and it had sections in Algeria, Paris and Madrid.

The French government and the GPRA signed a ceasefire in March 1962 and Algerians were granted the right to decide their own future. In the weeks before these events, in a desperate attempt to prevent their happening, the OAS heightened its terrorism, including firing mortar rounds into the Casbah in Algiers. The ZAA regrouped to retaliate. Indiscriminate killings then increased further: in May, an OAS car bomb killed 62 Algerian Muslims at the Algiers dock and the following week they reported killing 230 more. They also burned the University of Algiers Library.

The consequence of OAS terrorism was not its intended aim of returning Algeria to civil war, and thereby stopping Algerian independence, but the unintended panicked exodus of Europeans. As such, it was not so much that it lost the battle but more that, as a consequence of the battle, the end for which the battle was fought disappeared. Although the FLN succeeded, in the sense that Algeria eventually gained its independence, the use of terrorism was not the key to this success. The terrorism went out of the FLN's control;

The consequence of OAS terrorism was not its intended aim of returning Algeria to civil war, and thereby stopping Algerian independence, but the unintended panicked exodus of Europeans

no strategy was produced for emulation elsewhere. The clearest lessons to be drawn from the Algerian case are that terrorist groups lead to opposition terrorist groups and increasing state repression offers absolutely no guarantee of provoking mass insurrection. These were not, however, the lessons drawn by al-Fatah.

Recommended reading

Again, Martha Crenshaw, ed., *Terrorism in Context* (University Park, PA: Pennsylvania State University Press, 1995) has excellent contributions on some of these cases: David Scott Palmer, 'The Revolutionary Terrorism of Peru's Shining Path'; Paul Wallace, 'Political Violence and Terrorism in India: The Crisis of Identity'; Martha Crenshaw, 'The Effectiveness of Terrorism in the Algerian war'. David C. Rapoport, ed., *Inside Terrorist Organizations* (London: Frank Cass, 2001) also has valuable contributions on terrorism in Peru and in Palestine and Israel.

For full-length works, see David Scott Palmer, *The Shining Path of Peru* (New York: St Martin's Press, 1994);

M.R. Narayanswamy, *Tigers of Lanka: From Boys to Guerrillas* (New Delhi: Konarak, 1994); J.S. Grewal, *The New Cambridge History of India II.3: The Sikhs of the Punjab* (Cambridge: Cambridge University Press, 1990); Helena Cobban, *The Palestine Liberation Organization: People, Power, and Politics* (New York: Cambridge University Press, 1983); and Martha Crenshaw Hutchinson, *Revolutionary Terrorism: The FLN in Algeria, 1954–1962* (Stanford, CA: Hoover Institution Press, 1978).

CHAPTER 8

International terrorism

IN THE MODERN WORLD SOME international dimension is more or less bound to exist for even the most indigenous of terrorist groups. With the ease of transport and global communications it is hardly surprising that terrorist groups purchase supplies, such as weapons, from foreign sources and raise money from ex-patriot supporters, as, for example, the Tamil Tigers do. Given their nationalist goals, it is equally unsurprising that ETA has cells in the Basque region of France and that the IRA networks cross the borders between Northern and Southern Ireland. International terrorism, however, does not encompass terrorism that simply crosses borders or involves arms and finances obtained from abroad. It is not a variation of domestic terrorism, with a difference simply in degree; international terrorism is a different kind of terrorism.

To be engaged in international terrorism, a terrorist group must be involved in one or more of three things:

- the group must act together with at least one other terrorist group from another country;

- the terrorist act must be carried out abroad;

- demands made by the terrorists must involve negotiations with at least one foreign government.

International terrorism could not have taken off without modern technologies and infrastructure

International terrorism could not have taken off without modern technologies and infrastructure: the classic example is the hijacking of an airliner from one country to another with global communications used in negotiations and the terrorists belonging to groups from different continents. The timing of the arrival of international terrorism, however, was due not to technological inventions and innovations but to the political conditions of the late 1960s and, above all, to the Arab–Israeli War of June 1967 – the Six-Day War.

After June 1967

In the Six-Day War, the military forces of Egypt, Jordan and Syria were rapidly defeated. Up to that point Palestinian groups had confidence in Arab governments and their military forces achieving Palestinian liberation. As explained in the previous chapter, the quest for Palestinian liberation had developed within the various communities of Palestinian refugees that had resulted as a consequence of the founding of the State of Israel in 1948. The quest was embroiled in the competing quests of Arab countries to become leaders of the Arab world.

At a conference held in January 1964, hosted by Gamal Abdel Nasser, president of Egypt, the Palestine Liberation Organization (PLO) had been set up as the official Palestinian constituent of the Arab League. Its role was to be responsible for the liberation of Palestinians and the aim in setting it up was also to bring together the various Palestinian political and paramilitary groups that had developed, over the years, within the Palestinian refugee communities. The PLO Charter, issued in May 1964, included clauses directed at the destruction of Israel (clauses not removed until 1996). They also established a military force, the Palestinian Liberation Army. After the Arab defeat in June 1967, the Palestinian groups met together and, for some of the militants, the move away from reliance on Arab countries to deliver Palestinian liberation led towards the development of international terrorism.

The PFLP

George Habbash, leader of the Popular Front for the Liberation of Palestine (PFLP), which he founded in 1967 after the Six-Day War, recounted how the war completely changed his way of thinking. It led him, he explained, 'to adopt the Vietnamese model: a strong political party, complete mobilization of the people, the principle of not depending on any regime or government' (quoted in Cooley, 1997: 298). Habbash's mind-set was that of Israel as a colonial power in league with all capitalist imperial nations, the relationship much along the lines of that between Vietnam and US imperialism.

Habbash, a Palestinian Christian, had left Palestine in 1948 and settled in Lebanon. His intellectual group became part of the Arab Nationalist Movement (ANM), founded in Jordan in 1953. The ANM viewed Arab unity as necessary for Palestine to be restored: their cells were set up in Aden (the capital of today's Yemen), Kuwait and Libya and they also took part in operations controlled by Egypt in Gaza. In Syria, however, Habbash had been imprisoned. With Vietnam in mind, the PFLP sought not simply the establishment of a Palestinian nation state but a Marxist-style international revolution in which Palestine would be part of the new world order.

The PFLP's Marxist views on international revolution gave it common ground with Marxist groups elsewhere; this explains why joint RAF–PFLP terrorist acts would later take place. In December 1967, the PFLP operational commander, Wadi Haddad, made the argument for a change in tactics. In many ways it mirrored the contrasting positions taken in the late nineteenth century between the Marxist revolutionaries and the anarchists' 'propaganda by the deed'. Haddad argued for a move away from popular revolutionary combat against government forces to the dramatic action that would bring world attention to the Palestinian cause. He proposed the hijacking of an Israeli airliner.

> *Haddad argued for a move away from popular revolutionary combat against government forces to the dramatic action that would bring world attention to the Palestinian cause. He proposed the hijacking of an Israeli airliner*

The first such hijacking occurred on 22 July 1968: an El Al aeroplane (El Al is the Israeli national airline) en route from Rome, Italy, to Tel Aviv, Israel, was forced to land in Algiers, Algeria. Twelve Israeli passengers and crew were taken hostage and the event gained the Palestinians worldwide publicity.

The hostages were released in exchange for some Palestinian prisoners in Israel. The first killing occurred on 26 December 1968 when PFLP gunmen attacked an El Al aeroplane in Greece, at Athens airport: a man was killed and two other people were injured. Less than two months later, an exchange of fire took place between a PFLP team and an El Al security guard in Switzerland, at Zurich airport: it left the pilot and a terrorist dead and the co-pilot wounded.

On 29 August 1969, a TWA airliner (the United States' Trans World Airline) on flight from Rome to Athens, destination Tel Aviv, was hijacked and forced to land in Damascus, Syria. Leila Khaled, a Palestinian refugee who had joined the ANM when she was just 16 years old and had then trained with the PFLP, led the hijacking; she later described her actions as being carried out on the 'international battlefield'. Others copied the PFLP's example. In December 1969, three Arabs were arrested boarding a TWA airline in Athens, carrying not only guns and grenades but also a declaration that their actions were on behalf of the PFLP.

The following year, in July 1970, political conditions changed: President Nasser of Egypt agreed to a ceasefire with Israel. In response, the PFLP heightened its international terrorist campaign, seizing three aircraft on 6 September, hijacking one – a Pan-Am airliner – to Cairo, Egypt, where it was destroyed, and two – one a TWA airliner and the other Swissair – to Dawson's Field, an abandoned airfield in Jordan. These two aeroplanes were then added to by a third, a British BOAC plane, which was hijacked on 9 September, bringing the total held hostages at Dawson's Field to 300. Demands were made for the release of Palestinian terrorists held in jails in Israel and Europe. On

12 September the disembarked British and American planes were blown up with 54 Israelis and American Jews retained as hostages; the exchanges were made. In March 1971, the PFLP began its attacks in Europe, exploding Gulf Oil oil-tanks in Rotterdam, the Netherlands.

Al-Fatah and the PLO

Syria, where Habbash had been imprisoned, supported not the PFLP but al-Fatah.

Al-Fatah

Al-Fatah is an acronym, in reverse, for Harakat al-Tahir al-Watani al-Falistini, which translates as Palestine National Liberation Movement. The word *fatah* means 'conquest'. Al-Fatah was set up by Yasser Arafat in Gaza in 1955. The ideas behind the group were the Islamic values in line with those of the Muslim Brotherhood, which had been set up in Egypt in 1928. The guerrilla strategy adopted by al-Fatah drew on the example of the Algerian FLN, which succeeded in gaining independence from the French colonial power in 1962. Following the FLN victory Palestinians began to be trained for al-Fatah in Algeria. In 1963, after the coup d'état that brought the Ba'ath party to power there, al-Fatah moved its base to Syria.

Following the defeat in the Six-Day War, Arafat, like Habbash, had decided on a move away from reliance on Arab countries. Against the background of new paramilitary groups, fedayeen, springing up in the occupied territories, Yasser Arafat took the initiative, in October 1967, to go into the occupied West Bank and develop a network for resuming clandestine operations. In April 1968 Arafat was made the official spokesman of al-Fatah and in February 1969 he became chairman of the PLO.

Initially rejecting Haddad's move to international terrorism, in 1969 the PLO joined in. In October 1969, the Popular Struggle Front (PSF), one of the groups belonging to the PLO, exploded a grenade in the El Al office in Athens, killing one Greek child and wounding another. With the world's media focused on Jordan through the events of Dawson's Field, in September 1970 King Hussein took the opportunity to send the Jordanian army against the PLO bases in Palestinian refugee camps. Having killed thousands of fedayeen fighters, the Jordanian army succeeded in expelling the PLO from Jordan, in July 1971. With this defeat, September 1970 therefore became known as 'Black September'.

Black September

The name – the Black September Organization – was taken by a terror cell within al-Fatah, in which Arafat's deputy, Abu Iyad, was prominent. Although not formally part of al-Fatah, Black September not only had leaders from within the al-Fatah organization but also used its organizational structures.

In November 1971, Black September murdered the Jordanian prime minister while he was visiting Cairo and then, in December, its terrorists attempted to assassinate the Jordanian ambassador in London. Like the PFLP, Black September then turned its attentions on Europe, cooperating with the PFLP from 1972 to 1973. In February 1972, the PFLP hijacked a West German plane, a Lufthansa airliner, and successfully demanded a ransom of five million dollars from the West German government. At the PFLP's Third Congress, held in March 1972, Habbash succeeded in gaining a majority to reject, as he put it, 'operations outside Palestine'. Haddad refused to abide by the decision. In May 1972, Haddad used members of the Japanese terrorist group, the Japanese Red Army, to attack Lod airport in Israel. Using machine guns, the three Japanese terrorists opened fire in the airport lounge, killing 25 Israelis and wounding 78.

On 5 September 1972, Black September carried out its most outrageous act, this time against Israelis in Germany. During the Munich Olympics the terrorists stole into the Olympic village and entered building 31, where the Israeli team was housed. In the struggle, one of the athletes and a coach were killed and nine Israelis, a mixture of athletes and officials, were taken hostage. After negotiations with the German government, the hostages were taken to a nearby airport from whence the terrorists expected to be allowed to make their escape to Tunisia. When they discovered that they had been duped the terrorists killed all nine hostages and a German policeman. Black September next adopted the new tactic of sending letter bombs: an Israeli consul died as a consequence of one of them. At the end of October 1972, Black September hijacked another airliner, yet again one from the German airline Lufthansa. The hijacking secured the release of three of the surviving Black September terrorists from Munich.

Black September struck again in March 1973, this time in Sudan, where their terrorists took over the Saudi Arabian embassy in Khartoum. Not only did they demand the release of Palestinian prisoners in the West, including Robert Kennedy's assassin, but they also demanded the release of members of the Red Army Faction imprisoned in West Germany. None of the Western governments was willing to negotiate and so the Black September terrorists machine-gunned down three Westerners in the embassy compound: two Americans, one of whom was the US ambassador, and a Belgian diplomat. In September 1973, Black September terrorists attacked in France, where they took over the Saudi embassy in Paris. They demanded the release of a Palestinian terrorist in prison in Jordan. Again, they were unsuccessful. Black September's last appearance was in Italy, when, in September 1973, they attempted to shoot down an Israeli El Al airliner with ground-to-air rockets; Italian police foiled the attempt.

Following the Arab–Israeli War in 1973, al-Fatah formally renounced terrorism; Arafat wanted to be part of Middle East negotiations with the United Nations.

Following the Arab–Israeli War in 1973, al-Fatah formally renounced terrorism

The PFLP widens the international network

Black September ceased to operate but Haddad's PFLP terrorist group continued and developed further links leading to cooperation with terrorists in France, West Germany, Belgium and Holland. One of the most notorious international terrorists associated with the PFLP was 'Carlos the Jackal'.

Carlos the Jackal, 1949 –

'Carlos the Jackal' is the pseudonym of Illich Ramiréz Sanchez, a Venezuelan, born on 12 October 1949. A Marxist from a Marxist family, he spent time in both Cuba and the Soviet Union, where he attended the Patrice Lumumba University, Moscow, which specialized in providing communist education to developing world students. He developed connections with both the PFLP and European terrorist groups and, in June 1973, became the major PFLP organizer in Europe. In December 1973, he attempted to assassinate a top Jewish businessman in Britain and then carried out a bombing campaign in Paris. In January 1975, he attacked an El Al airliner at Orly Airport, Paris, using an anti-tank rocket launcher. The attack that brought him notoriety was carried out in Vienna in December 1975 against a meeting of 11 OPEC ministers. From late 1976 little was known of his whereabouts but he re-emerged, in 1983, with his Organization for the Armed Arab Struggle, which he both led and financed, to engage in a terror campaign. In January 1984, he bombed railways in France and French cultural centres in the capital cities of West Germany and Libya. He was finally captured, in August 1994, in Sudan.

Carlos the Jackal was widely believed to have led PFLP terrorists along with, possibly two, West German terrorists in an attack in Vienna, Austria, on 21 December 1975. Bursting into a meeting of OPEC (the Organization of Petroleum Exporting Countries), the terrorists killed 3 people, wounded 7 and took 81 people hostage, including all 11 of the ministers gathered to represent their countries. Threatening to kill their Iranian and Saudi hostages, the terrorists were given an aircraft and, having freed 41 Austrians, flew with their remaining hostages to Algeria. After releasing them, probably for a ransom as high as 50 million US dollars, they flew off. Their destination was thought to be Libya and it was alleged that Gaddafi had financed the Vienna attack for a sum equivalent to one million US dollars.

In June 1976, two PFLP members together with two members of the German Red Army Faction hijacked an Air France jet aeroplane at Athens Airport. Carlos the Jackal was alleged to have organized the attack. The aeroplane was forced to fly to Libya for refuelling and was then made to fly on to Entebbe, Uganda, where the crew and passengers were held hostage. The demands made were for the release of 53 terrorists held in various prisons around the world, including the leaders of the RAF in Stammheim prison. The terrorists failed; Israel's anti-terror squad succeeded in killing the terrorists without loss of life to the passengers kept hostage, with only one exception: one hostage unable to be located was left behind and killed on the orders of the Ugandan president, Idi Amin. On the terrorists' arrival in Entebbe, Amin had given his support to both their actions and their demands.

In October 1977, another PFLP–RAF team hijacked a Lufthansa airliner, landing it in Mogadishu, Somalia. This time West German paramilitary forces stormed the aircraft, again successfully. After this, PFLP terrorism fizzled out. In 1988, the PFLP complied with the al-Fatah position of confining action to Gaza and the West Bank.

Abu Nidal

Arafat's decision, after the 1973 Arab–Israeli War, that the PLO should enter negotiations with Israel through the United Nations led to factionalist fighting within al-Fatah and to splinter terrorist groups. The most prominent among these groups were those associated with Abu Nidal, who had been behind the Black September terrorist campaign. A Palestinian, Abu Nidal's real name was Sabri el-Banna and his role was that of representing Arafat in Iraq. El-Banna was opposed to Arafat's decision to enter negotiations with Israel. The Abu Nidal group first formed in Iraq in 1973, and in that year Abu Nidal helped the Libyan-based group Arab Nationalist Youth Organization (ANYO) to hijack a KLM airliner (KLM was the Dutch airline). In 1974, he set up Fatah – the Revolutionary Council, with Iraqi sponsorship; the group specialized in attacking moderate Palestinians in Arab countries and Israelis and Jews abroad. The Abu Nidal group also adopted other names: Al-Iqap against Saudi Arabian targets, the first in 1973; Black June against Syrian targets; the Egyptian Revolution or alternatively Revolutionary Egypt against Egyptian targets; Revolutionary Organization of Socialist Muslims (ROSM) against British targets; Revolutionary Arab Brigades (RAM) when attacking smaller Gulf states.

In 1980, Abu Nidal moved from Iraq to a new sponsor, Syria, from where Abu Nidal's 'People's Army', a militia not a terrorist group, played a part in driving the PLO out of Lebanon. The PLO therefore moved its base to Tunisia. From 1980, the number of terrorist attacks carried out by the Abu Nidal group rose: from no more than 5 a year in the 1970s, the attacks reached 30 or more in 1985. The balance of these attacks also shifted from selected assassinations to indiscriminate killings.

In December 1985, the Abu Nidal group attacked airports in Vienna and Rome. As tourists queued at the El Al ticket counters, Abu Nidal terrorists threw grenades into their midst and fired at them with sub-machine guns, killing 14 people and wounding 100. At the time, both Austria and Italy were prominently involved in European schemes to draw the PLO into a peace settlement. While Libya, where Abu Nidal had opened operations in 1983, was considered to have been behind the attacks in Vienna and Rome, Syria was considered to have been behind Abu Nidal's attempt to blow up an El Al airliner flying from Heathrow Airport, London, in April 1986. From that point Abu Nidal transferred operations entirely to Libya and returned operations to assassinations. International terrorism continued but was carried out by a plethora of other groups.

Euroterrorism

Euroterrorism was the name given to the spate of terrorism carried out by various terrorist groups in Europe in the 1980s. The attacks were directed at targets largely connected with NATO and Americans. The

Euroterrorism was the name given to the spate of terrorism carried out by various terrorist groups in Europe in the 1980s

start was in 1981 when a US army commander was kidnapped by the German Red Army Faction (RAF) and an American general was kidnapped by the Italian Red Brigades. In December 1984, the NATO Iberian Command was attacked, in Portugal, by a group calling itself the Forcas Populares 25 do April who then, in January 1985, attacked three NATO vessels with mortar-fire. In January 1985, the German RAF and Action Directe, the French terrorist group, announced that they had joined in their fight against NATO. In February 1985, Greek terrorists, the National Front group, exploded a bomb near Athens in a bar frequented by American soldiers: 78 people were injured, many of them

Americans. Also in late 1984 and early 1985, in Belgium, the Fighting Communist Cells (CCC) attacked the NATO pipeline system and bombed a NATO building in Brussels. A similar attempt was made on a NATO school in West Germany and in April 1985 the German RAF sabotaged a NATO pipeline, also in West Germany.

This spate of terrorism in Europe peaked in December 1984 and January 1985 following the start of a hunger strike, on 4 December 1984, by German RAF terrorists serving sentences in prison in West Germany; at this peak over 50 terrorist-related incidents occurred in Western Europe. The hunger strike was the ninth conducted by the RAF; the first had been in 1973. The December 1984 hunger strikes begun by two RAF prisoners had grown to 36 RAF prisoners by the time it was called off. In addition to other acts of sabotage and killings associated with the hunger strike, protesters in the Netherlands occupied the German embassy and brought an Amsterdam–Munich train to a halt, all to bring attention to the German hunger strikers. Outside Europe international terrorism also carried on, given new life by the Iranian Revolution.

Islamic terrorism after the Iranian Revolution

A new strand of international terrorism developed as a consequence of the Iranian Revolution of 1979: it brought the Islamic religion squarely into the foreground. As mentioned before, Hizbollah, the Shiite Muslim terrorist organization created and sponsored by Iran in 1982, emerged in Lebanon as one of the groups of the Islamic Jihad movement: the movement had splintered off from the Muslim Brotherhood in Egypt in

1967. Hizbollah's novelty was terrorist attacks carried out by young men with explosives strapped to their bodies, human bombs – suicide bombers. Having claimed responsibility in April 1983 for the attack on the US embassy in Beirut in which a suicide bomber in a lorry killed 63 people and injured a further 120, Islamic Jihad then carried out similar but this time simultaneous suicide bombings. On 23 October 1983, at the US marine barracks near Beirut airport, 241 marines were killed; at the nearby French barracks 58 soldiers were killed. The movement also claimed responsibility for the bombings of both the American and the French embassies in Kuwait, carried out in December 1983.

A new strand of international terrorism developed as a consequence of the Iranian Revolution of 1979: it brought the Islamic religion squarely into the foreground

Hizbollah, alone, claimed responsibility for the bomb attack carried out in April 1984 on a restaurant near Madrid, Spain, which killed 18 people and injured 83 others. Also, it was probably Hizbollah that carried out the hijacking of a TWA aircraft in June 1985, though the group's preferred tactic at the time was the taking of high-profile Western hostages. Terry Waite, the Archbishop of Canterbury's emissary, was one of those hostages. It was the year in which the highest total in any one year, 19, was reached. All the remaining hostages, for not all had survived, were released by the end of 1991. Hizbollah hijacked a Kuwaiti airliner in February 1988 and four years later they again hit the headlines. In March 1992, in retaliation for the assassination by Israeli commandos of Hizbollah's secretary general, Mousawi, his wife and child also killed in the operation,

Hizbollah terrorists exploded a car bomb outside the Israeli embassy in Buenos Aires, Argentina. The explosion killed 29 people and injured 240 others.

Coinciding with the peak of Hizbollah's high-profile foreign hostages, groups associated with the PLO returned to international terrorism, directing their attacks at tourists. In September 1985, Arafat's personal bodyguard, Force 17, attacked and killed three Israeli tourists on board a yacht in Cyprus. In October 1985, the Palestine Liberation Front (PLF) hijacked a passenger ship, *Achille Lauro*, on the coast of Egypt, taking over 700 people hostage and demanding the release of 50 Palestinian prisoners from Israel. In 1986, a disciplinary unit of the PLO, Hawari, also turned to international terrorism when Hawari terrorists placed a bomb on board a TWA airliner. In the *Achille Lauro* incident, the terrorists shot a defenceless, wheelchair-bound, 69-year-old man for no reason other than because he was an American Jew.

The bad publicity brought by the *Achille Lauro* incident led, once again, to Arafat denouncing PLO terrorism, this time in the Cairo Declaration of November 1985. In 1988, he publicly recognized the right of Israel to exist and, in 1993, the PLO and Israel's government signed the Oslo Peace Accord.

One of the consequences of Arafat and the PLO's changes in position was the *intifada* (popular uprising), which broke out in the West Bank and Gaza in December 1987 in protest against Israeli occupation. Another was that other terrorist groups emerged from within those territories claiming to act for the Palestinian people in competition with the PLO. The most important of these groups were Islamic Jihad, which was founded in Palestine in 1980 as part of the Islamic Jihad movement, and Hamas. Hamas is by far the largest of the groups.

Hamas

Hamas (acronym for *Harakat al-Muqawama al-Islamiyya*, Islamic Resistance Movement) was established in December 1987, straight after the eruption of the *intifada*, by a Palestinian Sunni group including the leader of the Muslim Brotherhood in Gaza, Sheikh Ahmad Yasin. In its charter, issued in August 1988, Hamas rejected the right to a state of Israel and called all Muslims to fight a holy war – jihad – for the establishment of a Palestinian Islamic state, one that is based on Islamic principles and Shari'a law. The *intifada* ended after the Israeli–Palestinian peace settlement, the Declaration of Principles (or Oslo Accords), were signed in September 1993; it agreed to interim self-government authority for Palestine leading to permanent status. From that point, however, Hamas began to work in opposition to the PLO and developed closer links with Iran.

From 1994, directing its attacks on Israelis and Palestinians within the rejected state of Israel, Hamas engaged in suicide bombings, with bus explosions and nail bombs their speciality. After the Hebron massacre, the shooting of Palestinians worshipping in a mosque carried out by a Jewish extremist in February 1994, which killed 29 people and wounded a further 150, a Hamas suicide bomber blew up a bus full of commuters in Afula killing 8 Israelis and wounding 50 more. Over the three years from September 1993 to 1996, Hamas suicide bombings killed more than 200 Israelis. In March 1997, one of their suicide bombers detonated a nail bomb in a crowded café in Tel Aviv, killing 3 Israelis and injuring 40 others.

During this time, international terrorism continued to be carried out by other Islamic groups. Bomb attacks, thought to have been carried out by Hizbollah, injured passers-by in London in 1994. In December 1994, the Algerian terrorist group Armed Islamic Group (GIA) hijacked an Air France Airbus in Algeria and forced it to fly to the south of France, demanding the release of terrorists held in French jails. All the terrorists but none of the 170 passengers were killed when the aircraft was stormed by French counter-terrorist troops. In July 1995, GIA set off a bomb in a Paris underground station, killing 7 people and injuring 84.

Back in 1993, however, a new phase of international terrorism had been opened by an Egyptian terrorist group – the Islamic Group – until then only associated with attacking tourist targets in Egypt. In February that year the Islamic Group exploded a huge bomb in the World Trade Center building in New York, killing 6 victims and injuring over 1,000 people. Among those arrested and convicted for the attack was Sheik Omar Abdel Rahman, the leader of the Islamic Group, who had been exiled to New Jersey, USA.

Transnational terrorism

In 1996, Osama bin Laden, leader of al-Qaida, issued from his base in Afghanistan a 'Declaration of War against the Americans'. At the heart of the justification for declaring war on the USA was the stationing of US forces in Saudi Arabia. In the text of the Declaration he said that it is viewed as the greatest act of aggression against Muslims since AD 632, the year in which the Prophet

In 1996, Osama bin Laden, leader of al-Qaida, issued from his base in Afghanistan a 'Declaration of War against the Americans'

Muhammad died. Osama bin Laden is Saudi Arabian. On 7 August 1998, al-Qaida carried out simultaneous car bomb attacks on the American embassies in Kenya and Tanzania. By 11 September 2001, when the hijacked aeroplanes flew into the twin towers of the World Trade Center in New York and the Pentagon in Washington, al-Qaida had a transnational network of cells with which miltant organizations had connections: in Algeria, Bangladesh, Egypt, Kashmir, Libya, Pakistan, Syria and Yemen. The membership of al-Qaida also consisted of diverse nationalities; those who have passed through the training camps in Afghanistan have included people from the Middle East to far east Asia, from north Africa and east Africa, from Europe and North America (Bergen, 2001).

Al-Qaida grew out of the Salifiyya, an Islamic religious movement that, like the Assassins centuries before, is committed to, as they see it, the pure Islam of the Prophet Muhammad and, therefore, to the shariah, the Islamic law. The terrorist groups Islamic Jihad and Hamas also grew out of the Salifiyya; Egyptian Islamic Jihad fully merged with al-Qaida. The Taliban in Afghanistan likewise grew out of the Salifiyya. In the Salafi view of the world modern Western civilization, in which the United States of America is seen as the most powerful Western nation, epitomizes the false idols that must be destroyed in the battle for pure Islam and the universal Islamic community, the *umma*.

The ideas held by al-Qaida are shared by only a very small minority of Muslims but, ironically in view of their anti-modern stance, through the dramatic events of '9/11' the group has been successful in exploiting the modern media to the full. The impression has been created of al-Qaida's great size, spread and organization, though information remains speculative and the best indications point to its being not a centrally directed but a loose organization. What lay behind the development of this new transnational Islamic terrorist group was, primarily, the Soviet withdrawal from Afghanistan in the late 1980s. Al-Qaida was set up some time in 1988 to 1989 in Peshawar, Pakistan, near the border with Afghanistan, in order to keep the disparate Islamic extremist groups that had been fighting against the Soviet army together as an 'international army' (Burke, 2003: 8).

Although the United States had supported the Afghan Moja-hedin both militarily and financially, al-Qaida cast America in the part set out in the Salifiyya. In al-Qaida's eyes, both America and the Soviet Union were part of the 'Zionist–Crusader alliance' who set up false idols. The important and influential Salafi thinker, Sayyid Qutb, writing in the 1950s, expressed the position in the following way:

In al-Qaida's eyes, both America and the Soviet Union were part of the 'Zionist–Crusader alliance' who set up false idols

. . . *the Crusader spirit that runs in the blood of all Occidentals. It is this that colours all their thinking, which is responsible for their imperialistic fear of the spirit of Islam and for their efforts to crush the strength of Islam. For the instincts and the interests of all Occidentals are bound up together in the crushing of that strength. This is the common factor that links together communist Russia and capitalist America. We do not forget the role of international Zionism in plotting against Islam and in pooling the forces of the Crusader imperialists and communist materialists alike. This is nothing other than a continuation of the role played by the*

Jews since the migration of the Prophet to Medina and the rise of the Islamic state.
(Quoted in Scott Doran, 2002: 139)

For those who held Sayyid Qutb's view, it was confirmed by the US-led invasion of Afghanistan after '9/11' and then by the invasion of Iraq. Others interpreted the events in terms of the fall of terror regimes.

Recommended reading

For a concise introduction to the Arab–Israeli conflict, see Kirsten K. Schulze, *The Arab–Israeli Conflict* (London and New York: Longman, 1999). On the PLO, see Helena Cobban, *The Palestine Liberation Organization: People, Power, and Politics* (New York: Cambridge University Press, 1983). On Islamic Jihad, see Ziad Abu Amr, *Islamic Fundamentalism in the West Bank and Gaza: Muslim Brotherhood and Islamic Jihad* (Bloomington, IN: Indiana University Press, 1994). For a comprehensive work on Islamic movements in Arab countries, see R. Hrair Dekmejian, *Islam in Revolution, Fundamentalism in the Arab World* (Syracuse, NY: Syracuse University Press, 1995). On Abu Nidal, see Patrick Seale, *Abu Nidal: A Gun for Hire* (London: Random House, Arrow edition, 1993), where the possibility of Abu Nidal being an Israeli agent is investigated.

On international terrorism in general, Robert O. Slater and Michael Stohl, eds, *Current Perspectives on International Terrorism* (London: Macmillan, 1988) offers a good set of contribtions, especially Alex Schmid, 'Goals and Objectives of International Terrorism'. On al-Qaida, Jason Burke, *Al-Qaeda: Casting a Shadow of Terror* (London: I.B. Taurus, 2003), Peter Bergen, *Holy War, Inc.: Inside the Secret World of Osama bin Laden* (London: Weidenfeld and Nicolson, 2001), and Faisal Devji, *Landscapes of the Jihad* (London: Hurst and Company, 2005) make very interesting reading, and Bergen has actually interviewed bin Laden.

Once again, *Keesing's Contemporary Archives* to 1987 (London and Harlow Keesing's Publications, Longman), re-named *Keesing's Record of World Events* from 1988 (Cambridge: Keesing's Worldwide), are excellent primary sources for all the examples of terrorism.

CHAPTER 9

The future of
terrorism

PAST, PRESENT OR FUTURE, terrorism remains a chosen
strategy implemented through a system of summary justice, its
essence the deliberate targeting of innocents as victims:

Emile Henry 'resolved the question' at his trial for terrorism in 1894:
'The building where the Carmaux Company had its offices was
inhabited only by bourgeois: hence there would be no innocent victims.'
(*Gazette des Tribunaux,* 27–28 April 1894, translated in
Woodcock 1977: 193)

Over a century later the following report of a trial appeared:

Members of a British terror cell talked about blowing up the Ministry
of Sound nightclub in London as a contribution to the global jihad, the
Old Bailey heard yesterday. One of the defendants, Jawad Akbar, said
the gang would not be blamed for attacking the club as they would be
targeting 'those slags dancing around' rather than innocent people.
(*Guardian,* 26 May 2006: 1)

No innocent victims, yet the club could hold up to 1,800 people.

But things have changed. The anarchist groups were clear in their political ends, their interpretation of socialism: propaganda by the deed was the means to destabilize the government and rally support for the overthrow of the existing bourgeois system. The lack of clarity in the goals of many of today's terrorist groups, anti-capitalist though not left wing, have some similarities with the New Left terrorist groups of late capitalist society in respect of their ambition to change social values and in their simplified doctrines. They are also like the right-wing terrorist groups in Italy at that time in their choice not to identify their group and not to express their demands, sometimes never to do so.

The more vague the political goals, the more bound up with religious ones, the more postmodern today's terrorist groups have become

The more vague the political goals, the more bound up with religious ones, the more postmodern today's terrorist groups have become. To set off a bomb, declare publicly the name of the group, the nature of the goals sought and the demands made is modern. Such acts give scope for rational calculation and negotiation. Set off a bomb and identify both the group and its goals, at best, only indirectly, and it is difficult to see how exactly the act is calculated to move towards ends. Seek ends in the afterlife and desires for changes on earth too general to be the basis upon which negotiations with governments can take place and the goal-orientated calculations of modern rational thought no longer apply. It is a fine aspiration for social and economic conditions to be improved in countries from whence this postmodern terrorism emanates but it is hard to be sure that such improvements would have any tangible effects in reducing terrorism. Such improvements are not declared goals and if greater social economic improvements were achieved other justifications, explanations and rationalizations would, no doubt, be brought to bear.

Religion, though, is not postmodern; it pre-dates modern, and it is antithetical to modern secularization, but knowledge of the past informs interpretation of the present. Understanding the rise of religious terrorism through the lessons of history could not predict '9/11' any more than it could have predicted the Stern Gang or the rise of the Khalistani Sikh terrorist groups. It had, though, the potential to provide the necessary insight for governments to cease their fixation on left-wing 'revolutionary terrorism' well before the fall of communism in Eastern Europe and the Soviet Union.

Lessons for countering terrorist groups

As the cases of terror regimes, reigns of terror and state terrorism have shown, abandoning the due process of law and using indiscriminate violence are the hallmarks of terrorism in governments. If terrorism is to be ended it must not be countered by terrorism in another form. As examples in liberal democracies have shown, too,

If terrorism is to be ended it must not be countered by terrorism in another form

repressive responses on the part of the government and violent responses on the part of state forces may lead to the formation of terrorist groups. In practice, furthermore, the effects of different government responses to terrorism demonstrate the positive advantages of sensitive rather than heavy-handed responses (della Porta, 1992).

In liberal democracies, the importance of sensitive hand-ling also applies to the media. As the lessons of history have also shown, and ironically so, democratic institutions, such as freedom of information, serve to facilitate terrorist groups. In consequence, the media in liberal democracies have an extra responsibility: in addition to that of reporting events they must also resist reacting in such a way as to exaggerate terrorist acts and so inflate their future threat. For, as has become clear, the aims of terrorist groups include that of gaining media coverage. Furthermore, as has also become apparent, terrorism as a polit-ical act involves in its calculation the production of reaction, not least by government; an important weapon against terrorism, therefore, is to react not in line with the terrorists' calculations but in an unexpected way. With continual innovation in strat-egies – from national to international and on to transnational networks – and tactics – bombs under benches, car bombs, aeroplane hijacking, suicide bombers, nerve gas, aeroplanes as bombs – countermeasures too must be innovative and tailored to each case. The advantages of modern technology that can be used to work for terrorism can also be used to counter it.

Lessons for ending state terrorism and regimes of terror

Defeat in foreign war brought an end both to Nazi Germany and to Pol Pot's Cambodia. The Vietnamese army together with the Cambodian National United Front for National Socialism, formed from the refugees who had fled to Vietnam over the intervening years, succeeded in defeating the Khmer Rouge in 17 of the 19 provinces of Cambodia. The People's Revolutionary Council was established in Phnom Penh in January 1979. A similar invasion, by the Tanzanian army and Ugandan exile forces, brought down Idi Amin's regime. In Argentina, General Galtieri's Junta was defeated in the Falklands War. In East Timor an Australian-led peacekeeping force arrived to end the terror. Such arrivals, however, offer no guarantees, as the arrivals of the Indian army in Sri Lanka and the British army peacekeeping forces to resolve the Troubles in Northern Ireland have also shown.

Foreign invasion is not the solution to all terror regimes and it can bring problems of its own: the case of Iraq is an obvious example. The major problem is that of ensuring a peaceful solution after the

> *Foreign invasion is not the solution to all terror regimes and it can bring problems of its own: the case of Iraq is an obvious example*

event. International law and international forces hold the potential to bring down terror regimes but the costs in both lives and money make this a difficult calculation to make for predicting the future of government terror. The case also illustrates the difficulties of knowing the extent of a regime's terrorism: whether approximating an exceptional system of terror, like that in Nazi Germany, or, rather, fitting that of more commonplace state terrorism.

In Chile, General Pinochet was removed by holding and losing an election in December 1989. The case illustrates not only another means for ending state terrorism nor simply that even bad things come to an end but also the inherent problem of prediction. New things happen. Who would have predicted after the coup in 1973 that Pinochet would one day lose office through an election? It was no more predictable than that Hamas would one day be elected to be the government in the Palestinian territories, as it was in January 2006. Or again, who predicted Libya's surprise declaration, in December 2003, that it was abandoning its weapons of mass destruction? But then who predicted '9/11'? Quite as unpredictable as the next act of the terror regime or the explosion of the terrorist's bomb. Who could not but be taken by surprise that on the very same morning that Saddam Hussein was hanged for crimes against humanity in Iraq, 30 December 2006, ETA, having agreed a ceasefire nine months earlier, exploded a bomb at Madrid Airport, injuring 19 people?

The uncertainties are too great to predict the future of terrorism in other than the broadest terms. With its long history, its capacity to develop new types and to utilize ever more lethal technologies, the odds are stacked on the side of terrorism continuing long into the future, most likely in some new and unpredictable forms. We can, though, hope that it will not and seek to guard the future against it.

References

Abu-Amr, Z. (1994) *Islamic Fundamentalism in the West Bank and Gaza: Muslim Brotherhood and Islamic Jihad*. Bloomington, IN: Indiana University Press.

Andics, H. (1969) *Rule of Terror*. London: Constable.

Arendt, H. (1958) *The Origins of Totalitarianism*. San Diego, CA: Harcourt Brace and Company.

Arendt, H. (1963) *On Revolution*. New York: Viking Press.

Arnson, C.J. (2000) 'Window on the Past: A Declassified History of Death Squads in El Salvador', in B.B. Campbell and A.D. Brenner (eds), *Death Squads in Global Perspective: Murder with Deniability*. London: Macmillan.

Bacon, E. (1994) *The Gulag at War: Stalin's Forced Labour System in the Light of the Archives*. London: Macmillan.

Bakhash, S. (1985) *The Reign of the Ayatollahs; Iran and the Islamic Revolution*. London: I.B. Taurus.

Bergen, P. (2001) *Holy War, Inc.: Inside the Secret World of Osama bin Laden*. London: Weidenfeld and Nicolson.

Broszat, M. (1968) 'The Concentration Camps, 1933–45', in H.B. Krausnick, H. Buchheim, M. Broszat, and H.-A. Jacobsen (eds), *Anatomy of the SS State*. London: Collins.

Brown, R.M. (1971) 'Legal and Behavioural Perspectives on American Vigilantism', *Perspectives in American History*, 5, pp. 93–144.

Bunyan, J. and Fisher, H.H. (1965) *The Bolshevik Revolution 1917–18*. Stanford, CA: Stanford University Press.

Burke, J. (2003) *Al-Qaeda: Casting a Shadow of Terror*. London: I.B. Taurus.

Burleigh, M. and Wippermann, W. (1991) *The Racial State: Germany 1933–1945*. Cambridge: Cambridge University Press.

Carney, T. (1989) 'The Organization of Power', in K.D. Jackson (ed.), *Cambodia 1975–1978: Rendezvous with Death*. Princeton, NJ: Princeton University Press.

Carr, E.H. (1966) *The Bolshevik Revolution 1917–23*, vol. 1. Harmondsworth: Penguin.

Cobb, R. (1987) *The People's Armies – the Armées Revolutionnaires: Instrument of the Terror in the Departments April 1793 to Floreal Year* II. New Haven, CT: Yale University Press.

Conquest, R. (1971) *The Great Terror: Stalin's Purge of the Thirties*. Harmondsworth: Penguin.

Conquest, R. (1990) *The Great Terror: A Reassessment*. London: Hutchinson.

Cooley, J. (1997) 'Middle Eastern Terrorism 1948–1969', in M. Crenshaw and J. Pimlott (eds), *Encyclopedia of World Terrorism*, vol II. Armonk, NY: M.E. Sharpe.

Crenshaw Hutchinson, M. (1978) *Revolutionary Terrorism: The FLN in Algeria, 1954–1962*. Stanford, CA: Hoover Institution Press.

Crenshaw, M. (1985) 'An Organizational Approach to the Analysis of Political Terrorism', *Orbis*, 29, pp. 465–89.

Crenshaw, M. (1992) 'Decisions to Use Terrorism: Psychological Constraints on Instrumental Reasoning' in D. della Porta (ed.), *International Social Movements Research: Social Movements and Violence: Participation in Underground Organizations*, vol. 4. Greenwich, CT and London: JAI Press Inc.

Dallin, D.J. and Nicolaevsky, B.I. (1948) *Forced Labour in Soviet Russia*. London: Hollis and Carter.

Debray, R. (1968) *Revolution in the Revolution?* Harmondsworth: Penguin.

Degregori, C.I. (1992) 'The Origins and Logic of Shining Path: Two Views', in D.S. Palmer (ed.), *The Shining Path of Peru*. New York: St Martins Press.

Della Porta, D. (1992), 'Institutional Responses to Terrorism: The Italian Case', *Terrorism and Political Violence*, 4, pp. 151–70.

Della Porta, D. (1995) *Social Movements, Political Violence, and the State: A Comparative Analysis of Italy and Germany*. Cambridge: Cambridge University Press.

Della Porta, D. and Tarrow, S. (1986) 'Unwanted Children: Political Violence and the Cycle of Protest in Italy, 1966–1973', *European Journal of Political Research*, 14, pp. 607–32.

Deutscher, I. (1968) *Stalin: A Political Biography*. Harmondsworth: Penguin.

Engene, J.O. (2004) *Terrorism in Europe: Explaining the Trends since 1950*. Cheltenham: Edward Elgar.

English, R. (2004) *Armed Struggle: The History of the IRA*. London: Pan Books.

Fairbairn, G. (1974) *Revolutionary Guerrilla Warfare: The Countryside Version*. Harmondsworth: Penguin.

Friedrich, C.J. and Brzezinski, Z.K. (1965) *Totalitiarian Dictatorship and Autocracy*. Cambridge, MA: Harvard University Press.

Gillespie, R. (1995) 'Political Violence in Argentina: Guerrillas, Terrorists, Carapintadas', in M. Crenshaw (ed.), *Terrorism in Context*. University Park, PA: Pennsylvania State University Press.

Greer, D. (1966) *The Incidence of the Terror during the French Revolution: a Statistical Interpretation*. Gloucester, MA: Peter Smith.

Gregor, J. (1982) 'Fascism's Philosophy of Violence and the Concept of Terrorism', in D.C. Rapoport and Y. Alexander (eds), *The Morality of Terrorism*. New York: Pergamon Press.

Guardian, 'Terror, Trial Hears Tapes of Plot to Blow up Club',
26 May 2006. Available online at: www.guardian.co.uk/
frontpage/story/0,,1783457,00.html.

Guevara, C. (1969) *Guerrilla Warfare*. Harmondsworth: Penguin.

Homze, E.L. (1967) *Foreign Labor in Nazi Germany*. Princeton, NJ:
Princeton University Press.

Iviansky, Z. (1977) 'Individual Terror: Concept and Typology', *Journal
of Contemporary History*, 12, pp. 43–63.

Ivianski, Z. (2001) 'The Terrorist Revolution: Roots of Modern
Terrorism' in D.C. Rapoport (ed.), *Inside Terrorist Organizations*.
London: Frank Cass.

Jackson, K.D. (1989) 'The Intellectual Origins of the Khmer Rouge',
in K.D. Jackson (ed.), *Cambodia 1975–1978: Rendezvous with Death*.
Princeton, NJ: Princeton University Press.

James, H.J. (1987) *The German Slump: Politics and Economics 1924–1936*.
Oxford: Clarendon Press.

Joshi, M. (1996) 'On the Razor's Edge: The Liberation Tigers of Tamil
Eelam', *Studies in Conflict and Terrorism*, 19, pp. 19–42.

Kannyo, E. (2000) 'State Terrorism and Death Squads in Uganda
(1971–79)', in B.B. Campbell and A.D. Brenner (eds), *Death Squads
in Global Perspective: Murder with Deniability*. London: Macmillan.

Keesing's Contemporary Archives, 1974–87. London and Harlow:
Keesing's Publications, Longman.

Keesing's Record of World Events 1988–. Cambridge: Keesing's
Worldwide.

Kiernan, B. (1996) *The Pol Pot Regime: Race, Power, and Genocide in
Cambodia under the Khmer Rouge, 1975–79*. New Haven, CT: Yale
University Press.

Landau, R.S. (1992) *The Nazi Holocaust*. London: I.B. Taurus.

Leggett, G. (1981) *The Cheka: Lenin's political Police*. Oxford: Clarendon
Press.

Llera, F.J., Mata, J.M. and Irvin, C.L. (1993) 'ETA: From Secret Army to Social Movement – The Post-Franco Schism of the Basque Nationalist Movement', *Terrorism and Political Violence*, 5, pp. 106–34.

McClintock, C. (1984) 'Why Peasants Rebel: The Case of Peru's Sendero Luminoso', *World Politics*, 37, pp. 48–84.

McCormick, G.H. (2001) 'The Shining Path and Peruvian Terrorism', in D.C. Rapoport (ed.), *Inside Terrorist Organizations*. London: Frank Cass.

Marighela, C. (1971) *For the Liberation of Brazil*. Harmondsworth: Penguin.

Markakis, J. and Ayele, N. (1978) *Class and Revolution in Ethiopia*. Nottingham: Spokesman.

Melson, R. (2003) 'Modern Genocide in Rwanda: Ideology, Revolution, War, and Mass Murder in an African State', in R. Gellately and B. Kiernan (eds), *The Specter of Genocide: Mass Murder in Historical Perspective*. Cambridge and New York: Cambridge University Press.

Melucci, A. (1981) 'New Movements, Terrorism and the Political System: Reflections on the Italian Case', *Socialist Review*, 56, pp. 97–136.

Merkl, P. (1995) 'West German Left-Wing Terrorism', in M. Crenshaw (ed.), *Terrorism in Context*. University Park, PA: Pennsylvania State University Press.

Nove, A. (1993) 'Victims of Stalinism: How Many?', in J.A. Getty and R.T. Manning (eds), *Stalinist Terror: New Perspectives*. Cambridge: Cambridge University Press.

Palmer, D.S. (1995) 'The Revolutionary Terrorism of Peru's Shining Path', in M. Crenshaw (ed.), *Terrorism in Context*. University Park, PA: Pennsylvania State University Press.

Quinn, K.M. (1989) 'Explaining the Terror', in K.D. Jackson (ed.), *Cambodia 1975–1978: Rendezvous with Death*. Princeton, NJ: Princeton University Press.

Rapoport, D.C. (1984) 'Fear and Trembling: Terrorism in Three Religious Traditions', *American Political Science Review*, 78, pp. 658–77.

Roxborough, I., O'Brien, P. and Roddick, J. (1977) *Chile: The State and Revolution*. London: Macmillan.

Rummel, R.J. (1990) *Lethal Politics: Soviet Genocide and Mass Murder since 1917*. New Brunswick, NJ: Transaction Publishers.

Schultz, R. (1978) 'The Limits of Terrorism in Insurgency Warfare: The case of the Viet Cong', *Polity*, 11, pp. 67–91.

Scott Doran, M. (2002) 'Somebody Else's Civil War', *Foreign Affairs*, 81, pp. 22–42.

Sprinzak, E. (1995) 'Right-Wing Terrorism in Comparative Perspective: The Case of Delegitimation', *Terrorism and Political Violence*, 7, pp. 17–43.

Stirling, C. (1981) *The Terror Network: The Secret War of International Terrorism*. New York: Holt, Rinehart and Winston.

Taylor, J.G. (2003) 'Encirclement and Annihilation: The Indonesian Occupation', in R. Gellately and B. Kiernan (eds), *The Specter of Genocide: Mass Murder in Historical Perspective*. Cambridge and New York: Cambridge University Press.

Trotsky, L. (1961) *Terrorism and Communism*. Ann Arbor, MI: Ann Arbor Paperbacks, University of Michigan Press.

Vickery, M. (1985) *Cambodia, 1975–1982*. London: Allen and Unwin.

Viola, L. (1993) 'The Second Coming: Class Enemies in the Soviet Countryside, 1927–1935', in J.A. Getty and R.T. Manning (eds), *Stalinist Terror: New Perspectives*. Cambridge: Cambridge University Press.

Wallace, P. (1995) 'Political Violence and Terrorism in India', in M. Crenshaw (ed.), *Terrorism in Context*. University Park, PA: Pennsylvania State University Press.

Woodcock, G. (1977) *The Anarchist Reader*. Glasgow: Fontana/Collins.

Zawodny, J.K. (1981) 'Infrastructures of Terrorist Organizations', *Conflict Quarterly*, 1, pp. 24–31.

Index

'9/11' 1, 4, 6, 8, 14, 27, 183, 185, 189, 192
26 July Movement 39–41, 42

Abu Iyad 171
Abu Nidal (Sabri el-Banna) 176–7
Abu Nidal groups 175–7
Action Directe 177
Action for National Liberation (ALN) 44
Afghanistan 182, 183, 184, 185
al-Fatah (Palestine National Liberation Movement) 22, 160, 163, 170–73, 175
Algeria 22, 45–7, 160–63, 168, 170, 174, 182, 183
Battle of Algiers 46, 161
Algerian National Liberation Front (FLN) 22, 45–7, 160–63, 170
Allende, Salvador 105, 112, 113
ALN *see* Action for National Liberation
al-Qaida 4, 6, 8, 182–5
see also '9/11'
Amin, Idi 24, 108, 175, 191

Amir, Yigal 9
anarchism 14–17
Anarchists 14–20, 62, 188
Arab Nationalist Youth Organization (ANYO) 176
Arab–Israeli war
of 1973 173, 175
First 159
Six-Day War (June 1967) 167, 166–8, 170
Arab Nationalist Movement (ANM) 167–8, 169
Arafat, Yasser 160, 170, 175, 176, 180
Arendt, Hannah 72, 73, 81
Argentina 191
terrorist attack in 118, 180
and Triple A 106–7, 112–13
Armed Islamic Group (GIA) 182
Armenia, massacres in 99–100, 102
assassinations 7–8, 9, 14, 16, 17, 19, 45, 68, 126, 136, 137, 146, 148, 149, 158, 160, 171, 173, 174, 176, 177, 179
Assassins 7–8, 9, 22, 28, 34, 183

Aum Shinri-Ky 9
Austria 116, 174–5, 176, 177

Baader, Andreas 132–3, 134, 139
Baader-Meinhof Gang/Group *see*
    Red Army Faction
Ba'ath Party 100, 170
Basque Movement for National
    Liberation (MLNV) 129
Basque Separatists *see* ETA
Belgium 173, 178
Bhindranwale, Sant Jarnail Singh
    152–3, 154, 155
bin Laden, Osama 182–3
Black September 116, 171–3
Bolsheviks 19, 20, 51–2, 61, 62,
    63, 78
Bosnia 102
Brazil 43–4, 143
Brigate Rosse see Red Brigades
Britain/British *see* United
    Kingdom
Burundi 99, 102

Cambodia 12, 75, 83–5, 91–4,
    190–91
  see also regimes of terror,
    in Cambodia; totalitarian
    regimes, in Cambodia under
    the Khmer Rouge
Carlos the Jackal 116, 173–4, 175
Chechen terrorists 2
Cheka (Commission for
    Combating Counter-
    revolution and Sabotage)
    52–3, 62–3
Chile 105, 112, 191

China 21, 39, 53, 72
CIA (US Central Intelligence
    Agency) 112, 113
civil rights movement in Northern
    Ireland 124, 127, 131, 139
civil war 39, 59, 60–61, 62, 63–4,
    65, 66, 69, 86, 90, 91, 92, 101,
    123, 125, 150, 159, 162
collectivization 12, 65, 76, 77, 88,
    92
Committee of General Security 31,
    49, 50
Committee of Public Safety 10, 31,
    50, 51
communism 71, 114, 184, 189
  see also Communist Party;
    Marxism/Marxist; Soviet
    Union, and the communist
    network
Communist Party 20, 21, 39,
    147
  of Brazil 44
  of Cambodia 84, 85
  of Chile 113
  of Germany 130, 131
  of Indonesia 103
  of Iran (Tudeh Party) 68
  of Italy 135, 137
  of Peru 144
  of the Soviet Union 20, 63
  see also Bolsheviks
concentration camps
  Armenia 99
  Bosnia-Herzogovina 102
  Ethiopia 54, 55
  Germany 75, 80–81, 82, 91
concept of terrorism 27–48

countering terrorist groups 189–90

coup d'état 83, 92, 100–101, 102, 103, 105, 106, 108, 170

Croatian separatists 37

Cuba 21, 39–41, 42, 53, 72, 114, 115, 174

Cyprus 180

Dawson's Field 169–70, 171

death squads and disappearances 55, 64, 102, 103–10, 150

Debray, Regis 42–3

dekulakization 74, 75, 76, 88

democracy 5–6, 17, 112, 113–14, 139, 143, 144, 145, 146, 147, 150, 190
see also terrorist groups, from within liberal democracies

Democratic Kampuchea see Cambodia

Derg (Co-ordinating Committee of the Ethiopian Armed Forces, Police and Territorial Army) 53–4

Deutsche Aktionsgruppe 23

dictatorship see terrorist groups, and repressive regimes; totalitarian dictatorship

disappearances see death squads and disappearances

dislocated society 85–6, 86–7, 91–3

dynamite 14, 37, 38

Earth First! 37

East Timor 103–4, 191

Easter Rising 21, 123

economic crisis 59–60, 61, 62–3, 65–6, 67, 86, 87, 88–90, 93
renewed
in Cambodia 93–4
in the Soviet Union and Germany 88–90

Egypt 158, 159, 160, 166, 168, 169, 170, 178, 183
terrorist attacks in 3, 176, 180, 182

El Salvador 108, 109–10

ending state terrorism and regimes of terror 190–92

enemies see real enemies versus innocents

England 53
terrorist attacks in 2, 4, 123, 127, 174, 177

Ensslin, Gudrun 132–3, 134, 139

Eritrea 63–4, 65–6

ETA (Euskadi 'ta Askatasuna, Basque Homeland and Freedom) 21–2, 115, 116, 122, 127–9, 138, 140, 165, 192

ETA-M (ETA-Militar) 128–9, 138, 139

ETA-PM (ETA-Político-Militar) 128

Ethiopian Revolution 53–6, 63–6, 67

ethnic cleavages/differences 102, 107, 108, 135, 144, 146, 147, 148, 149, 150, 151–6, 157–9, 160–61
see also holy terror; Islamic terrorism after the Iranian Revolution; Northern Ireland

Euroterrorism 177–8
Ezhov, Nikolai 78, 79

FALN (Armed Forces for Liberation) 22
fascism 23, 28–9, 100, 121
fascist state 131, 132, 135
  see also Italy, fascist regime in
Fatah – the Revolutionary Council 176
fedayeen (Palestinian) 160, 167, 170, 171
Feraoun, Mouloud 47
First World War 23, 62, 86, 100
FLN see Algerian National Liberation Front
Force 17 180
foreign war 59, 61, 64–5, 66, 67, 86, 87, 91, 92, 93, 190, 191
  see also Arab–Israeli War; First World War; Second World War; Vietnam War
formation of terrorist groups 138–40, 189
France 84, 46, 47, 73, 156–7, 160–63, 165
  terrorist attacks in 18–19, 36, 46, 173, 174, 182
freedom fighters 38, 39
  see also guerrilla armies/groups/ movements, terrorist versus freedom fighter
French Revolution 9, 10–11, 12, 31–2, 49–51, 59–61, 63
  see also revolutionary reigns of terror, in France
future of terrorism 187–92

Gaddafi, Muammar 116, 175
Gaza (Strip) 118, 157, 159, 160, 168, 175, 180, 181
gelignite, development of 14
genocidal campaigns see massacres and genocidal campaigns
  see also Holocaust
genocide 99, 107, 134
Germany
  East Germany 130
  under Hitler/Nazi Germany 12, 23, 35, 72, 73, 74, 157, 158, 190, 191
  Imperial 62, 156
  terrorist attacks in 116–17, 172
  Weimar 62, 87, 89
  West Germany 20, 23, 24, 129–35, 138–9, 156, 171, 173, 174, 175, 178
Gestapo 80
Golden Temple complex at Amritsar 152, 154, 155
GPU (State Political Administration) 63, 75, 76, 77
Great Purges (Great Terror) 12, 32–3, 35, 78–9, 89, 90
Greece 24, 37, 169, 175, 177–8
Guatemala 107, 112
guerrilla armies/groups/ movements 21, 38, 39, 44, 92, 106, 107, 109, 123, 144
  foco 21, 39–41, 43
  rural 38, 39, 43, 144
  terrorist versus freedom fighter 37–48
  urban 42, 43–4, 68

guerrilla warfare 38, 39, 68, 128, 160

Guerrilla Warfare 41–2

Guevara, Ernesto ('Che') 41–2, 43

GULAG 75

Gulag system/camps 33, 75–7, 79

Guzmán Reynoso, Abimael 144–5, 146–7

Habbash, George 167, 168, 170, 171

Haddad, Wadi 168, 172, 173

Hamas (Islamic Resistance Movement) 9, 118, 180, 181, 183, 192

Henry, Emile 18–19, 36, 121, 187

Hezbollah, Iran 58

hijacking 1, 24, 37, 134, 166, 168–9, 171, 176, 180, 183, 190

Himmler, Heinrich 80, 81

Hitler, Adolf 12, 34, 37, 73, 81, 89, 90, 158

Hizbollah, Lebanon 117, 178–9, 182

Ho Chi Minh 44

Holocaust 130, 135

see also regimes of terror, in Germany; totalitarian regimes, in Hitler's Germany

holy terror 6–10, 28, 188–9

see also ethnic cleavages/ differences; Islamic terrorism after the Iranian Revolution; Northern Ireland

hostages 2, 24, 36, 37, 133, 168, 170, 172, 174, 175, 179

Hussein, Saddam 100–101, 192

Hutu Power 97, 98

Hutus 97, 98, 99

ideology 14, 23, 27–8, 72, 100, 121, 133

see also anarchism; communism; fascism; Marxism/Marxist; National Socialism; nationalism; socialism

India 149, 150, 183, 191

terrorist attacks in 2, 3–4, 9, 148–9, 150–56

Indonesia 2, 8

under Suharto 103–4

industrialization 86, 87, 88

innocents as victims 1, 4, 16,19, 39, 41, 43, 73, 74, 79, 83, 100, 104, 107, 114, 139, 140, 187

in Cambodia 93–4

in Germany and the Soviet Union 90–91

see also victims; violence, against innocents

intifada (popular uprising) 180, 181

international state terrorism 112–18

international terrorism 24–5, 160, 165–86

intimidation 72, 106

contrasted with terrorism 29–31, 33, 35

IRA *see* Irish Republican Army; Official Irish Republican Army; Provisional Irish Republican Army

Iran 8, 56–9, 101, 131
  and international state
    terrorism 117–18, 181
Iranian Revolution 53, 56–9,
      66–9, 117, 178
  see also Islamic terrorism after
    the Iranian Revolution
Iraq 57, 157, 176, 192
  under Saddam Hussein
      100–101, 102, 118, 185, 191
  terrorist attacks in 3
Ireland 21, 123, 138, 154, 165
  see also Northern Ireland
Irgun Zvai Leumi 158–9
Irish Republican Army (IRA) 21,
      115, 116, 122, 123–7, 138,
      140, 165
Islamic Group 182
Islamic Jihad movement 117, 178,
      179
Islamic Jihad (Palestinian) 9, 118,
      180, 183
Islamic Republican Party (IRP) 58,
      67, 68
Islamic Republic see Shia Islamic
    Republic
Islamic Revolutionary Guard
      (IRG) 58, 67, 68, 117
Islamic terrorism after the Iranian
    Revolution 178–82
Ismali Inqilabi Mahaz 8
Israel 9, 24, 117, 158, 159, 166,
      167, 168, 169, 172, 175, 176,
      180, 181
  terrorist attacks in 3, 181
Italy 14, 20, 23, 129, 135–7,
      138–9, 168, 169, 173

  fascist regime in 20, 33–4, 35,
      72, 129
  terrorist attacks in 116, 176,
      177

Jacobins 9, 10, 59, 60, 62
  see also revolutionary reigns of
    terror, in France
Japanese Red Army 172
Jemaah Islamiah (JI) 2, 8
Jihaz Haneen 100
Jordan 157, 159, 160, 166, 167,
      169, 171, 173
  terrorist attack in 3
June Second Movement (Bewegung
      2. Juni) 134

Kenya 183
Khaled, Leila 169
Khalistani Sikh groups 9, 151–6,
      189
Khieu Samphan 84, 92–3
Khmer Rouge 12, 83, 92, 93, 191
Khomeini, Ruhollah Mousavi
      56–7, 67, 68, 118
Kosovo 102
Kropotkin, Peter 15
Krystallnacht (Crystal Night) 81,
      90
Ku Klux Klan 22–3, 111
Kurds 67, 68, 99, 100, 101
Kuwait 101, 168, 194

labour camps 33, 76, 77, 88, 90,
      91, 104
  see also concentration camps;
    Gulag system/camps

Lashkar-e-Taiba 4
Lebanon 117, 118, 157, 167, 176, 179
left-wing terrorist groups 20–21, 114, 136, 188, 189
  see also New Left terrorism
Libya 24, 168, 174, 175, 177, 192
  and international state terrorism 115, 116–17
Lockerbie, Scotland 117
LTTE (Liberation Tigers of Tamil Eelam) 3, 22, 147–51, 165

MacGuire, Marie 139–40
Mao Zedung 39, 144, 147
Marighela, Carlos 43–4, 143
Marxism/Marxist 20, 113, 114, 121, 139, 168
Marxist parties 19
  see also Bolsheviks; Communist Party
massacres and genocidal campaigns 47, 93–4, 96, 97–102, 146, 181
media and terrorism 4, 6, 13, 24, 25, 121, 168–9, 171, 183, 190
Meinhof, Ulrike 132–3, 134
Mengistu Haile-Miriam 54–5, 56, 64
Middle East 9, 115, 134, 156–60
military regimes 102, 103, 106
Milosovic, Slobodan 101–2
modern terrorism 14–21, 188
  see also anarchists
Moro, Aldo 137
Morozov, Nicholas 16

Muslim Brotherhood 160, 170, 178, 181
Mussolini, Benito 72, 135

Narodnaya Volya see People's Will
Nasser, Gamal Abdel 160, 166, 169
National Liberation Front (NLF) 44–5
National Socialism 23, 35
  see also NSDAP; regimes of terror, in Germany; totalitarian regimes, in Hitler's Germany
nationalism 21–4, 128, 165
  see also terrorist groups, and nationalism
Nazi Party see NSDAP
Netherlands 173, 178
Nicaragua 53, 113
New Left terrorism 129–40, 138–9, 188
NKVD (People's Commissariat for Internal Affairs) 77, 78, 79
NLF see National Liberation Front
Norkabal 85
Northern Ireland 21, 123–7, 131, 138, 139–40, 165, 191
North Korea 115
NSDAP (National Socialist German Workers' Party) 79, 80, 89–90, 130, 135, 157
Nuclei Armati Rivoluzionari 23

Official Irish Republican Army (OIRA) 125–6, 127
Oklahoma City bombing 122

Organisation d'Armée Secrète
(OAS) 46, 162
organization of terrorist groups 5,
8, 25, 35, 121, 140–41, 149,
155–6, 162, 171, 183–4

Pakistan 151, 183, 184
Palestine 73, 134, 166–71, 181,
192
Ancient 6–7, 34
under British mandate 157–9
Palestine Liberation Front (PLF)
180
Palestine National Liberation
Movement *see* al-Fatah
Palestinian Liberation
Organization (PLO) 22,
166–7, 170–71, 175, 176,
177, 180, 181
Panunzio, Sergio 28–9
peacekeeping 125, 150, 191
People's Will (*Narodnaya Volya*)
16–17, 19–20, 141
Peru 144–7
PFLP (Popular Front for the
Liberation of Palestine) 22,
24, 134, 167–70, 171, 173–5
Pinochet, Augusto 105, 112, 191,
192
PIRA *see* Provisional Irish
Republican Army
Pirabhakaran, Velupillai 148
PLO *see* Palestinian Liberation
Organization
PMAC (Provisional Military
Administrative Council) 54,
65

Pol Pot 12, 75, 83, 84, 85, 93,
190
Portugal 177
Popular Front for the Liberation of
Palestine *see* PFLP
propaganda by the deed 14–16,
25, 35, 43, 133, 143, 161,
168, 188
Provisional Irish Republican
Army (PIRA) 21, 125–7,
138–40
Puerto Rico 22
Punjab 9, 150–56

Qutb, Sayyid 184–5

real enemies versus innocents
28–9, 35–7, 39, 45
see also innocents as victims
Red Army Faction (RAF) 20,
24, 36, 115, 116, 122, 129,
130–35, 138–9, 168, 175,
177, 178
Red Brigades (*Brigate Rosse*) 20,
115, 116, 122, 129, 135–7,
138–9, 177
Red Terror, Ethiopia 55, 56
regime terrorism, varieties of
11–14
see also regimes of terror;
state terrorism; totalitarian
regimes
regimes of terror 13, 31–4, 97,
120, 121, 143, 185, 189
in Cambodia 12
in Germany 12, 20, 71
in the Soviet Union 12, 20, 71

see also ending state terrorism and regimes of terror; revolutionary reigns of terror; totalitarian regimes

reigns of terror *see* revolutionary reigns of terror

religion *see* ethnic cleavages/ differences; holy terror; Islamic terrorism after the Iranian Revolution; Northern Ireland

repressive regimes 33, 72, 106, 128
  see also terrorist groups, and repressive regimes

revolutionary reigns of terror 49–70, 71, 96, 189
  definition 69
  in Ethiopia 12, 53–6, 63–6
  explaining 59–69
  in France 10–11, 49–51, 59–61, 131–2
  in Iran 12, 56–9, 66–9
  in Russia 12, 51–3, 61–3

Revolutionary Tribunal/ revolutionary tribunals
  in France 31, 32, 34, 49–50, 51
  in Russia 52

right-wing terrorism in Italy 136–7, 188

Ríos Montt 107

Robespierre, Maximilien 10, 50, 51, 63

Russia
  post-Soviet, terrorist attacks in 2, 3
  Tsarist 15–17, 19–20, 86, 100
  see also Soviet Union

Russian Revolution 15, 19, 20, 51–3, 61–3, 86

Rwanda 12, 97–9, 102, 103

Sabotage 37, 41–3, 55, 78, 123, 146, 178
  distinguishing from terrorism 41–4

Saudi Arabia 176, 182

SAVAMA 58, 67

Schleyer, Hanns-Martin 36, 133

secret police 72, 73, 89
  see also Cheka; Gestapo; GPU; Jihaz Haneen; NKVD; Norkabal; SAVAMA; SS; Stasi

Second World War 23, 71, 82, 158

Sendero Luminosa (the Shining Path) 21, 38–9, 143, 144–7

Serbia 102

Shia Islamic Republic 67, 68, 117

Shining Path *see* Sendero Luminosa

socialism 14, 114, 188

Socialist German Students' Association (SDS) 132, 133

Socialist Revolutionary Party (SR) 19, 20, 62

Somalia 64–5, 175

Soviet Union 12, 20, 32–4, 35, 71, 72, 74, 86, 87, 88–9, 174, 184
  and the communist network 114–16
  see also regimes of terror, in the Soviet Union; totalitarian regimes, in Stalin's Soviet Union

Spain 21, 127–9, 138, 139, 162, 179
  terrorist attacks in 2, 4, 192
Special Boards (Special Tribunal), Soviet Union 33, 77, 78
Special Tribunal for the Defence of the State, Italy 33
Sri Lanka 3, 147–51, 191
  see also LTTE
SS 33, 34, 36, 80, 81, 82, 91, 100
Stalin, Josef 12, 32, 65, 71, 75, 76, 83, 88, 92
Stammheim Prison, Stuttgart 133, 175, 178
Stasi 115, 116
state terrorism 96–119, 161, 189
  see also death squads and disappearances; ending state terrorism and regimes of terror; international state terrorism; massacres and genocidal campaigns; vigilante groups
Stern Gang 9, 158–9, 189
Sudan 118, 172–3, 174
Suharto, T.N.J. 103
suicide terror attacks/terrorists 1, 2, 3, 7, 22, 141, 148, 149, 179, 181, 190
Switzerland 169
system of terror 9, 35, 69, 72, 83, 91, 96
  in Cambodia under the Khmer Rouge 83–5
  in Hitler's Germany 79–83
  in Stalin's Soviet Union 75–9

Syria 8, 100, 117, 118, 156, 166, 168, 169, 170, 176, 177, 183

Tamil Tigers see LTTE
Tanzania 183, 191
terror regime see regimes of terror; totalitarian regimes
terrorism
  definition 9, 48, 187
  past and present 1–26
  see also concept of terrorism; countering terrorist groups; future of terrorism; holy terror; international state terrorism; international terrorism; Islamic terrorism after the Iranian Revolution; modern terrorism; New Left terrorism; regime terrorism, varieties of; regimes of terror; revolutionary reigns of terror; right-wing terrorism in Italy; sabotage, distinguishing from terrorism; state terrorism; terrorist groups; totalitarian regimes; transnational terrorism
terrorist groups
  from within liberal democracies 120–42
  and nationalism 21–4, 124, 128
  and repressive regimes 143–64
  see also countering terrorist groups; formation of terrorist groups; future of terrorism; holy terror; international terrorism; left-wing terrorist

groups; modern terrorism;
New Left terrorism;
organization of terrorist
groups; right-wing terrorism
in Italy; terrorism, past and
present; transnational
terrorism
Thugs 8, 9, 13, 28, 34
totalitarian dictatorship 72, 73,
129
totalitarian regimes 71–95, 96,
129
in Cambodia under the Khmer
Rouge 83–5, 91–4
in Hitler's Germany 79–83, 87,
89–91, 129, 130
in Stalin's Soviet Union 75–9,
86–9, 90
towards explanation for
85–94
see also regimes of terror
transnational terrorism 182–5
Triple A (Anti-Communist
Alliance of Argentina)
106–7
Trotsky, Leon 61
Tunisia 97, 98, 99
Tuol Sleng 85
Turkey 3, 57, 99, 100, 101, 156
Turkish Seljuk Empire 8, 34
Tutsis 97, 98, 99

Uganda 98, 99
under Idi Amin 24, 108, 175,
191
United Kingdom 123–7, 156–7,
158, 174, 176, 191

see also England; Ireland;
Lockerbie, Scotland; Northern
Ireland
United States of America 22–3,
24, 44–5, 53, 73, 92, 93, 101,
117, 122, 183, 184
and international state
terrorism 112–14
terrorist attacks in 1, 2, 4, 22,
122, 167, 182, 183, 184–5
see also '9/11'
vigilantism in 22–3, 110–12

victims
of regimes of terror/totalitarian
regimes 32–4, 76, 78–9, 82–3,
83, 85
of revolutionary reigns of
terror 10–11, 12, 13, 31–2,
51, 52–3, 54, 55–6, 57, 58,
59
of state terrorism 12, 97,
99–100, 101, 102, 103, 105,
106, 107, 108, 109, 111
of terrorist attacks 1, 2, 3, 4,
116–17, 118, 122, 126–7,
134, 136–7, 139, 146, 148–9,
153–5, 156, 158–9, 162, 169,
171, 172, 174, 175, 176–8,
179, 180, 181
Vietnam 21, 44–5, 98, 167, 168,
190–91
Vietnam War 44, 45, 92, 129, 131,
134
vigilante groups 96, 109, 161
see also United States of
America, vigilantism in

violence 21, 28, 29, 60, 72, 125,
126–7, 135, 136, 138, 139,
143, 145, 147, 149, 151,
152–3, 154, 157, 159, 161,
170
  against innocents 28–31, 45,
  189

war see Arab–Israeli War; civil
war; First World War; foreign
war; Second World War;
Vietnam War
West Bank 118, 157, 159, 170,
175, 180

World Trade Center, New York 1,
36, 182

Yemen 183
  South Yemen 115
Yugoslavia under Slobodan
Milosovic 101–2

Zealots-Sicarii 6–7, 8, 9, 16, 28,
34
ZOG (Zionist Occupation
Government) 23–4
Zone Autome d'Alger (ZAA) 46,
161, 162